Spires of Faith

Historic Churches of Chicago

McGraw-Hill, Inc.
College Custom Series

*New York St. Louis San Francisco Auckland Bogotá
Caracas Lisbon London Madrid Mexico Milan Montreal
New Delhi Paris San Juan Singapore Sydney Tokyo Toronto*

McGraw-Hill's **College Custom Series** consists of products that are produced from camera-ready copy. Peer review, class testing, and accuracy are primarily the responsibility of the author(s).

Cover and title page photo of Holy Family Church (1857) courtesy of Michael A. Marcotte.

1 2 3 4 5 6 7 8 9 0 BKM BKM 9 0 9 8 7 6 5

ISBN 0-07-036063-4

Editor: Reaney Dorsey
Cover Design: Maggie Lytle
Printer/Binder: Bookmart Press

Dedication

To my wife Lynn, who is my shadow historian, for her encouragement and support, my parents, Joseph and Vivian Wolf, for their start, two special guys, Smiley and Doodle, and to Rose Wood, Epi, and the Luster sisters, true examples of history's best.

Wayne L. Wolf

I gratefully dedicate my artistic effort herein to my wife Margie without whose love many things would not have been possible and to Sister Marie Stephen Reges and Father Anthony Vader—my personal spires of faith.

Jack Simmerling

To my mother who gave me life, my father who gave me all of his camera equipment, my sister who gave me her dark room, my two significant friends, Frank and Diane, whose unconditional love and support keep me going, and finally to Wayne Wolf who gave me the opportunity to be a part of this project.

Miriam Kravis

Table of Contents

Introduction

Europeans came to America and brought with them cultural diversity and a religion matured by two millennia of growth and dispersion. They cared about their faith, gave their churches a generous portion of their meager factory wages, and retired daily to the crowded tenements surrounding their jobs. On Sundays, they dutifully tramped to their neighborhood church—a symbol of splendor in a sea of row houses. Pride adorned their faces as they gazed upon the stained glass, marble baptismal fonts, hand carved, intricate altars and gold spires pointing heavenward to the everlasting home they all would call their destiny. They spoke Italian, German, Polish, Russian, Spanish and countless other dialects and brogues. They all shared a common sacrifice to make Holy Family, St. Maurice, St. Sabinas, St. Columbanus, old St. Patrick's and dozens of other parishes showcases for their culture and their faith.

From the arrival of William Quarter, Chicago's first Catholic bishop, in 1844, the Docese of Chicago (later Archdiocese) devoted itself to building exemplary architectural houses of worship. Each bespoke a quiet elegance and tribute to the neighborhood it served, the faithful it ministered to, and the educational and social mission it imparted. By 1855, St. Henry's, St. Michael's, St. John the Baptist, St. Patrick's, and St. Francis Assisi joined St. Mary's in trying to expand fast enough to serve the seemingly endless waves of faithful immigrants pouring into Chicago from the East Coast and Europe. Suddenly, the expansion was halted by the great Chicago Fire of October 9, 1871. The Catholic parishes of Chicago suffered the same vast devastation wrought upon the city. One million dollars of blackened ashes lay where the parish houses, monasteries, and schools had once been. Bishop Thomas Foley spoke of the daunting future task of Chicago Catholics when he said they, "Have shown courage and energy [in rebuilding] their fine academies, colleges, schools, magnificent church edifices and other institutions [which] are among the chief ornaments of this city...."

Many of these "ornaments" still survive today, vibrant reminders of the faith and sacrifice that built them and still sustains them. This book is designed as a living architectural pilgrimage of some of Chicago's finest churches. They represent a kaleidoscope of nationalities, styles and magnificence, but together they chronicle a people and the faith in their city.

Wayne L. Wolf
Jack Simmerling
Miriam Kravis

Part One

The Early Years, 1849-1889:
From Bishop Quarter to Archbishop Feehan

"Chicagoans have traditionally taken much of their sense
of neighborhood from their parishes."

----*Catholicism: Chicago Style*

Holy Name Cathedral
735 N. State Street, Chicago, Illinois

Holy Name Cathedral, the home of Chicago's bishops, archbishops and cardinals since the mid-1800s, began as a small chapel on the campus of St. Mary of the Lake University. There on the second floor the English speaking parishoners felt at home and preferred to worship there than their assigned German parish of St. Joseph's. However, as happened in so many parishes during the boom time of Chicago's European immigration, the chapel quickly became too small to serve the growing number of English speaking residents. Thus, the Rev. Jeremiah Kinsella, President of St. Mary of the Lake University, obtained permission from Bishop Van de Velde to construct a larger, wooden church on the northeast corner of Superior Street and State St. The new church was quickly built and formal dedication services were held on November 18, 1849. Holy Name parish finally had achieved its own identity and its first resident priest, the Rev. William Clowry.

The frame church was enlarged twice in 1851 and 1852, but could still not keep up with the flux of new immigrants. A new permanent brick church was soon on the drawing boards. By August 3, 1853, the cornerstone of Holy Name was laid "Amid a vast concourse of people, Protestant as well as Catholic," and the great new church was begun. Milwaukee brick was imported, stained glass windows depicting scenes from the Bible were purchased, and stone for the walls was hauled in for the erection of the massive Gothic cathedral. When finished, the new church, built through the generous giving of the faithful, had topped the $100,000 mark, a princely sum in Chicago's frontier days. But the end product was imposing with the building measuring 196 feet long and 82 feet wide and the steeple soaring 248 feet above the base. The first frame church became classrooms for the Male Free School connected to the parish. Both this school and the St. James Female Free School, which was under the direction of the Sisters of Mercy, flourished.

In 1856 Bishop O'Regan contracted with the Fathers of the Holy Cross to assume responsibility for the church. They accepted this role but limited their educational attachment to a boys high school and male grammar schools at Holy Name and three neighboring parishes. The Sisters of the Holy Cross established an industrial school in the University and a girls school in a nearby rented building. Within five years, the Sisters gave up their direction of the girls school and it became a boys grammar school under the Christian Brothers. And shortly thereafter in 1861, the Holy Cross Fathers likewise withdrew from Chicago. The Rev. John McMullen then began the revitalization of St. Mary's of the Lake as a University adding schools of law, medicine and divinity. But the revitalized university with its new Rush Medical College, was also to succumb to diocesan infighting. It again closed in 1866, to be reopened as an orphan asylum. The orphanage flourished until both it and the church were destroyed by the great Chicago Fire of 1871. An eyewitness described the devastation in these poignant words, "As I stood there, the great unfinished spire of the Holy Name began to lurch eastward in the terrible heat... in an instant the roof was ablaze. The building seemed to melt down in front...."

Holy Name was not to vanish however. Funds for the rebuilding of the church were solicited throughout the United States and finally enough were received to hire New York architect Patrick C. Keely to make Holy Name a grand cathedral again. The cornerstone was laid on July 19, 1874 and the building commenced. When completed, it would become the largest church then in the city sporting, "A long vestibule, broad aisles and massive pews." The new cathedral was 216 feet long and 102 feet wide at its transpts. The spire was 210 feet high. The interior is itself a masterpiece where the visitor can see massive marble columns, a ceiling covered in intricate wood paneling, gold leaf embellishments that are fitting for a king, and 1500 electric lights to illuminate the rich interior colors. Much of the embellishment was accomplished by Mr. Scattaglia of Philadelphia and served as a fitting adjunct to the architectural work of Willett and Pashley of Chicago.

But the interior expansion was not complete. In 1914 the sanctuary was enlarged by architect Henry J. Schlacks who severed the eastern part of the church, moved its massive altar fifteen feet away, constructed new walls, a roof and floor, and a new baptistry was born. The church was done growing but not remodeling. After another five decades of use and abuse, Cardinal John Cody announced in 1968 that the cathedral had become structurally unsound and ordered a complete restoration. Spearheaded by the architectural firm of C.F. Murphy & Associates and the International Institute of Liturgical Art, the interior was gutted, a reinforced steel and concrete foundation was laid, and the sanctuary was rebuilt. A beautifully hand carved new main altar was carved from red-black granite by noted Argentinian sculptor Eugenio de Courten. De Courten's altar, weighing nearly six tons, was placed on a pedestal surrounded by cast bronze sculptures. Stations of the cross, also cast in bronze by Goffredo Verginelli, were hung on the exterior walls, and Milanese stained glass windows were installed throughout the cathedral. Sculptured bronze doors by Albert Friscia greeted the faithful as they came to worship. A new baptistry chapel, designed by Vittorio di Colbertaldo, was added to the side cathedral edifice. When completed, the 1970 church brochure proudly welcomed the return to the, "Continuity and purity of the Gothic design, the superfluous stucco decorations...were eliminated, along with multi-colored decorations, including murals in the upper area of the nave (which were replaced with Rosso Levanto marble). The hanging chandeliers were removed to enhance the beautiful vaulted ceiling....All new artwork was done in either bronze or marble to obtain a decorative unity of design."

The cathedral reopened on December 24, 1969 and since then has grown to over 1,000 families, has hosted Pope John Paul II, has heard the voice of Luciano Pavarotti echo from its loft, and has quietly seen the Sisters of Charity of the Blessed Virgin Mary maintain their vigilance over the education of the parish children. Good times and bad times have brought this former chapel to glory as Chicago's cathedral and it stands today as a symbol of all the architectural glory that has existed under the auspices of the Archdiocese of Chicago.

Even today, the spire of Holy Name, while not as tall as surrounding buildings, seems to soar to heaven with the joy of the faithful who gave for its construction and decoration.

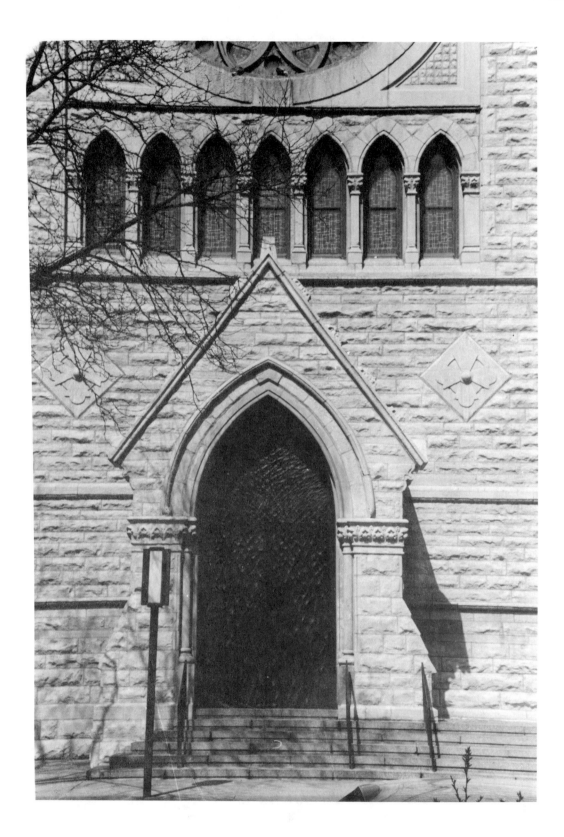

A side entrance to Holy Name Cathedral is highlighted by a massive carved door, an arched entrance and eight small windows.

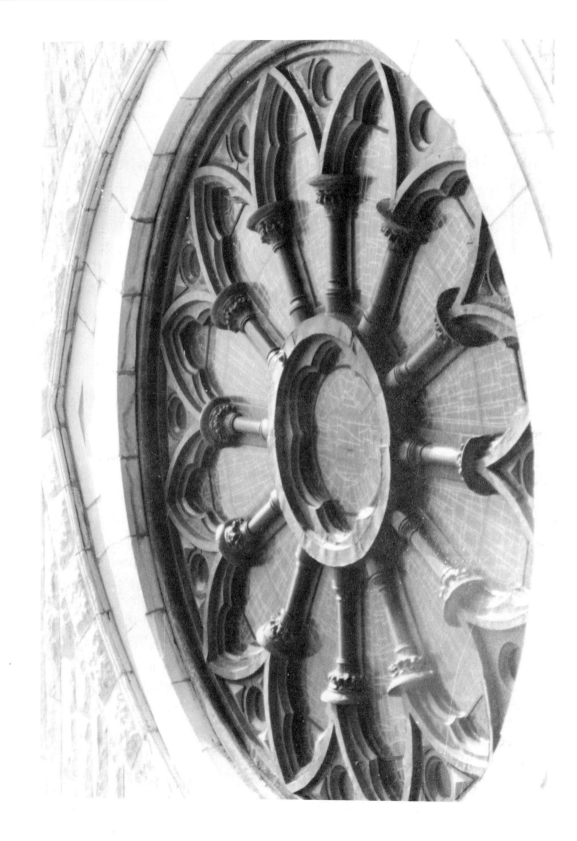

The stained glass window over the front entranceway of Holy Name Cathedral highlights both the artists craft and the beauty of the glass reflecting the sunlight.

Holy Family Church
1080 W. Roosevelt Road, Chicago, Illinois

In 1857, Bishop Duggan of Chicago was faced with a rapidly growing congregation of poor, working-class Irish immigrants who were then settling on the fringes of incorporated Chicago. The housing for these immigrants, in "desolate and uninviting localities," today akin to slums, had no plumbing, generally no heat, and poor ventilation. Even the breezes from Lake Michigan had a difficult time penetrating the narrow spaces between the tenements. This was the group of disadvantaged, frequently the subject of "riots and ructions," most affected by the Panic of 1857, which many likened to America's first Great Depression. Banks were closing, trade was at a virtual standstill, and hard currency was almost unobtainable. These obstacles however proved but a new challenge for Father Arnold Damen, S.J. when he was assigned to form a parish and build a church in this new Holy Family neighborhood, populated by poor Irish immigrants and fringed by prairies, wood frame homes, and belching factories. With this bleak financial picture, it was not expected that Father Damen could scrape together more than a few thousand dollars, build a frame church, and struggle for the next few decades. His letter of July 19, 1858 lamented, "Had I $6,000 I could make all payments and put the roof on the church." This was far from his design however. Rather, he energetically went about gaining over $30,000 in pledges, building a quick, temporary church, and immediately setting out to plan the permanent structure which was eventually to serve 20,000 parishioners and become the largest English speaking parish in the United States.

Father Damen lost no time in creating his dream. The cornerstone was laid on August 23, 1857 and the church completed and dedicated by Bishop Duggan on August 26, 1860. The *Chicago Tribune* called Father Damen, "The Hercules who has in a few years wrought all this work. To his energy, his ability, his sanctity, his perseverance, and his great practical intelligence is due not only the erection of this magnificent edifice but the great spiritual success which has crowned the labors of the Society." Magnificence may have been an understatement, for two additions by 1866 brought the total church dimensions to 186 ft. x 125 ft. The architectural style of the new church was attributed primarily to Mills Van Osdel and partially to the early work of Dillenburg & Zucker of Milwaukee. The primary style was Victorian Gothic, with brick trimmed by Illinois cut stone. Father Damen specified that the brick work was to be of the "best possible character, every joint filled solid with good lime and clean Lake Shore sand mortar." It was in the words of historian James W. Sanders, "The single great Irish workingman's parish." More importantly, the style—plain, heavy, massive and vaulted—revealed but one side of the workingman's composition of the parish. The other side was its sensitivity, its implicity, and its commonality which took those attributes the Irish workingman lived with and elevated them to a magnificent scale.

By luck, or divine intervention, Holy Family met its first great challenge during the Great Fire of 1871. It won. Its stained glass windows, vaulted ceilings, carved wood and marble, altar screen and organ survived. It stood as a beacon to the faithful in a sea of charred ash. And then it prospered. Italians arrived and joined the congregation in great numbers. Later African-Americans and Latino families joined the faithful. The names of Brown, Jackson, Martinez and Bray replaced Spoleto, Santucci, O'Brien and Collins. But together they built a solid, but shrinking, base of support for the church. But nature too took its toll over the years and the cracks of time began showing.

A leaky roof and interior plaster damage forced the closing of the church building in 1984. The stolid congregation was not going to give up however. In 1988, Father Robert Wild, Provincial General of the Society of Jesus, authorized the establishment of an independent, not-for-profit corporation with its sole objective the "restoring, managing and maintaining" of Holy Family Church.

This task would not be easy. Three million dollars was needed for the necessary repairs to meet safety and health codes and an additional million for an operating fund. While the fund raising continued, the faithful met in a small, plain room behind the main altar. The prayers have been successful. While the need for funds is a never-ending burden on the small urban congregation, their struggle to save one of Chicago's landmarks has thus far been a success. The church still survives, a tenuous but majestic inhabitant of Chicago's West Side.

Holy Family Church, 1080 W. Roosevelt Rd., Chicago, Ill. and the abuting St. Ignatius High School. Photos courtesy of Michael Marcotte.

A view from the choir loft draws the worshipper to the light and majesty of the main altar.

The magnificent main altar at Holy Family Church. Photo courtesy of Michael Marcotte.

A wonderful view of the interior vaulted aisle of Holy Family Church.
Note the ornately carved pillars.

"Satan Subdued" might be an appropriate name for this intricately carved statue at Holy Family Parish. Photo courtesy of Michael Marcotte.

St. Anne's
Renamed St. Charles Lwanga
55th & Wentworth, Chicago, Ill.

Father J.M. Kelly, the pastor of St. James Church of Chicago, recognized by 1865 that his parish was rapidly spreading south across the open prairies of Chicago and that a mission located to the south of St. James was urgently needed. Father Bowles was thus directed to establish the first St. Anne's in 1869—a small, frame building originally used as a Jewish synagogue that was moved to its new home on 55th Street and Wentworth Ave. From this temporary site, the first pastor, Fr. Thomas Leyden, shepherded his growing flock so that by 1875 a new permanent structure was necessary.

At this time, the *Chicago Tribune*, in its August 16, 1875 edition, described the future St. Anne's as follows:

> It will be rather unostentatious in its style of architecture, but very sufficiently ornamented
> to relieve it from austere plainness.

Thus with these broad outlines in mind, the cornerstone was laid by the Right Rev. Thomas Foley, D.D. and construction continued unabated until its completion on July 11, 1880. The final cost was $40,000.

Over the next few decades, the principally Irish parish grew from a vast prairieland to a bustling residential enclave of faithful. As the neighborhood filled with new parishoners, so did St. Anne's school. Originally built in 1890, it graduated countless civic leaders, musicians, priests and teachers to serve future generations. Thus, St. Anne's thrived for about three decades until its white parishoners left for points further south and the suburbs and the black immigrants owed their allegiance to other denominations. By the 1940s and 1950s, the frame and brick bungalows were lying vacant and boarded up. Shortly, those north of Garfield Boulevard were demolished to be replaced by public housing. In an effort to revitalize the church, the Archdiocese in 1971 renamed St. Anne's after a 20 year old Ugandan martyr executed for his faith in 1886, St. Charles Lwanga. But the precipitous decline could not be stopped. The Archdiocese could no longer afford the $400,000 annually to subside the parish. Thus in 1990 Cardinal Joseph Bernadin shuttered the church.

A brief respite came that same year when Dan Taylor, a minister with the Hope for the City Ministry, purchased the church, rectory and two adjacent buildings. Pastor Taylor's dream however was short lived. Unable to raise the nearly one million dollars necessary for repairs, he stood before the 150 foot spire, the magnificent 26 foot high entranceway where a rose window once formed the facade's centerpiece, and beneath a four foot copper cross (now green with age), and watched the Nicholas Frantation Construction Company swing its 3,000 pound wrecking ball. It was Tuesday May 10, 1994, the wreckers made the sign of the cross, and St. Anne's again returned to the vacant prairie lot it had been in 1875.

The graceful tower spire (150 feet high) and the intricate stone work of St. Anne's (St. Charles Lwanga) prepare to return their dust and stone origins in 1990.

The final destruction of St. Anne's (St. Charles Lwanga) in May of 1990. The nearly $1 million in repairs could not be raised.

An eerie view down the main aisle (looking north) during the May 1990 destruction. The spired bell tower is seen in the upper left.

The destruction of St. Anne's nearly complete, the scene is reminiscent of a bombed out city of World War II. (May 1990)

Holy Trinity Church
1118 N. Noble, Chicago, Illinois

Holy Trinity parish did not enjoy the same massive support and instant rise to success that many of its neighbors did. As a parish it was first organized in 1873 on Chicago's near northwest side, the center of Chicago's Polonia, to serve the needs of a large, diverse, mostly Polish congregation. Archdiocesan authorities opened and closed the parish several times because of serious controversies regarding Polish identity, control of church finances, and parish or congregation control and title to property over the ensuing two decades and finally decided on June 5, 1893, after the visit of the Apolostolic Delegate Francis Satolli, to create a permanent church for the parishioners in their neighborhood, their "trojcowo." Father Casimir Sztuczko, C.S.C. was appointed its first pastor.

Father Sztuczko found his new parish virtually in a shambles—the church was a plain wooden structure reminiscent of frontier outposts, the traditional attached school was nonexistant, and the weather conditions inside the church were identical to those outside. Almost immediately, the spirit of accomplishment reared its head and the parish began to come together. A new school designed by Polish architect John Wierzbieniec, suddenly rose three stories high and could accommodate 720 students. The total cost was $35,377.68. (In 1916 a new elementary school was erected with thirty-five classrooms and built of dark red brick, iron and concrete in an "L" shape). The old church was remodeled and two new twin tower bells were purchased. This was intended however as a temporary move as the number of parish families continued to grow rapidly. By 1905, the faithful had collected $48,100, the architectural firm of William Krieg had modified earlier plans and had gained Archdiocesan approval, and in April of 1905 the foundation was laid.

Today the parish church, of mixed Romanesque style, with twin towers, a Greek Acropolis-like entranceway, and solid lines stands as a tribute to what poor immigrants can do for their faith. Their magnificent church was painstakingly built of pressed brick, iron and limestone—materials designed for durability. But ornamental was not to be a missing concept. While the exterior shows large areas of plain, strong sections topped by three sectioned windows, there are ornate carvings depicting biblical figures, spires, scroll work and railings of fine workmanship and design. The twin bell towers bespeak a rising strength of form and simplicity and crown the glory of those early pioneers who made this Polish church the pride of the neighborhood.

Holy Trinity Church showing its mixed Romanesque style and
Greek entranceway flanked by twin bell towers.

The intricate side doors of Holy Trinity. Note the solid wood doors, biblical carvings, and twin spires accenting the curved molding.

A side view of Holy Trinity accents the strong lines, massive open spaces and series of miniature spires, denoting strength and reaching for heavenly acceptance.

St. Pius V
19th and Ashland Avenues, Chicago, Illinois

The Rev. Hugh McGuire, an Irishman and a Jesuit, was charged by the Archbishop of Chicago with establishing an Irish parish for those new immigrants in a pocket near the Polish parish of St. Adalbert. The area chosen was at 19th and Ashland Ave., on the city's near south side. The parish started by borrowing an existing school (St. Veronica) which had been opened by the Sisters of Charity of the Blessed Virgin Mary two years earlier and renaming it St. Pius and by constructing a frame church nearby at Van Horn and Paulina. As was so typical of these decades of high immigration, within two years Fr. McGuire was forced to enlarge the frame church and the following year (1908) add a new four story brick school at 1718 W. 18th Pl. He also purchased the property at the current church site, built a fine rectory, and began the planning for the present beautiful church. It was, however, to be his successor, Father Francis Henneberry, who in 1885 was to actually supervise the construction of St. Pius church. He commissioned the architect James J. Egan to draw up plans for the brick church at its present location.

As was also typical in the last few decades of the 20th Century, once plans for a church were drawn up, construction began in earnest almost immediately. Thus, on September 6, 1885 Archbishop Patrick Feehan was able to lay the new cornerstone. And by November 29, 1885, with only the basement completed, he dedicated the church. Construction was swift in those days but never compromised the structural integrity, its functionalism, or its strength. In May 1892 contracts were let for the final phase of construction and completed by September 10, 1893, the day of its dedication.

What the parishioners had built was sturdy, simple in design, but massive and stately in its effect on the neighborhood. The front entranceway and two side entrances display beautiful wooden doors, layered arched entrances, and stained glass semi-circular door crowns which admit the morning's light down the main aisle. A four story spire, topped with a stone cross which matches the cross of the front facade, exhibits straight lines but lovely narrow, elongated windows and alcoves—three on the second level, two on the third, and three more on the fourth. All are topped by three circular windows in the apex directly beneath the spire's cone. Perhaps the one area where ornamentation was allowed the workers was the front entrance atop the stone side panels. These were intricately carved column capitals and the brick over the entrance is rounded and tri-layered, each layer progressively more recessed. The carved front wooden doors contain eight panels each and use heavy wood, perfectly complimenting the brick and stone of the sides and stoop. This church was truly built to last decades as a lasting tribute to those early Irish immigrant workers.

By 1898 the new church was serving over 900 families and the parish building and grounds were appraised at $250,000, quite a feat in less than two decades. Over 1,000 children attended the parish school. By 1920 these numbers had reached 2,000 families but school attendance had dropped to 620 children, as many of the founding Irish families moved further south and southwest. The immigrant group to take their place was the Polish, with a few additional new families of Bohemian and Croatian ancestry. With this new ethnicity came a new control for St. Pius. Archbishop Mundelein invited the Dominican priests to take charge of the church and named the Rev. Albert Casey,

O.P. as pastor. The Dominicans brought two essential ingredients to St. Pius—their ability to speak Polish and a missionary zeal for new converts and service to the community. Both of these traits enabled the parish to prosper and grow. By 1925, enrollment again increased to 875 students, parish organizations had been revitalized, and the church was undergoing a transformation from an extensive remodeling. A shrine was added in honor of St. Jude, a marble altar replaced the old wooden one, and a chapel in honor of St. Anthony was erected in the church, all in the days of the Great Depression. The newly revitalized church served its parishioners well for the next several decades.

By the mid-1960s, another ethnic change was occurring at St. Pius. Large number of Hispanic Catholics were moving into the homes of the Eastern European founders. This new wave of immigrants brought additional changes to St. Pius. Masses were now offered in Spanish, the school curriculum was modified to stress individualized and bilingual instruction, and the commercial high school was closed. The number of elementary school children dropped to 253 by 1970. As with its neighbor St. Procopius, St. Pius also installed a shrine in honor of Our Lady of Guadelupe. Likewise, the church adopted the use of murals to depict daily life in Mexico, veneration of St. Jude, homage to Our Lady of Guadelupe, and the plight of Hispanic immigrants. These are located on the walls at the rear of the church, across the street, and on nearby neighborhood buildings. They help in defining the church and the neighborhood, not only as a place of worship but a memory of the homeland these new immigrants left looking for economic gains and freedom—the same goals sought by their Irish, German, Polish and Bohemian predecessors. The parish, through its elementary school and adult night classes, spreads the word of God along with the English skills essential to success in a new land. A new vibrancy thus characterizes an old immigrant parish, still serving those who come in search of a better life.

St. Pius V is highlighted by its magnificent bell tower, soaring four stories and
crowned by a spire and stone cross.

The magnificent carved wooden, eight panelled doors of St. Pius are recessed into a brick entranceway bordered on each side by lovely carved and ornamented faux columns.

Above one of the arched doorways to St. Pius is a beautifully carved coat of arms.
Note the classic arched and elongated windows separated by columns of white stone.

St. Pius parish has been an ardent supporter of mural art to decorate the neighborhood and simultaneously show off the culture of Mexico and the pride of Hispanic-Americans.

St. Margaret of Scotland
9837 S. Throop, Chicago, Illinois

Bishop Foley, faced with a burgeoning southside immigrant population, authorized the founding of St. Margaret's in 1874. Initial services were held in a small brick church at 95th & Throop Streets, a structure which now houses the chapel of the Academy of Our Lady High School. As was customary at the time, a new parish needed a new school for the educational component of a parish was viewed as the family anchor to the support and prosperity of the parish as a whole.

Father Bruno Riss, O.S.B., the first pastor, thus contacted nuns from the Sisters of Notre Dame to establish the first school, which opened November 1, 1874. The school, as did the parish, flourished, soon outgrowing their quarters. Thus, in 1894, Father McDonnell, the pastor, built a two story frame church and school structure to do double duty. In 1916, a three story brick rectory was added, and by 1919 St. Margaret's School was boasting 450 registered pupils.

Today, the church and school continue to serve the south side faithful. Over 2,000 families call this parish home and close to 270 students are enrolled in the school still taught by the School Sisters of Notre Dame. Fr. Mallette, the current pastor, now ministers to a congregational that is 60% African American and 40% white with Irish still being the largest European ethnic group.

St. Margaret's of Scotland is a wonderful example of the use of brick and concrete to weave intricate designs symbolic of crosses. Its twin spires and connecting facade of carved arches culminate in a cupola beneath which is the Virgin Mary in flowing robes and crown.

The apex of the facade of St. Margaret of Scotland shows the statue of the Virgin Mary sitting atop a carved portico and sheltered by a cupola. The oval "eye" below appears to be guarding the faithful and watching their daily endeavors.

St. Vincent de Paul
1010 W. Webster St., Chicago, Ill.

The dream and the need for St. Vincent de Paul began in August of 1875 when five acres of cow pasture, vegetable gardens and weed prairies was purchased. No wonder it was affectionately termed "Father Smith's Farm" after the priest who began the building in October 1895. The first church, intended to be temporary, was actually a combination school and church, with the former occupying the first floor and the latter the second. The first mass was celebrated by Father Smith on December 25, 1875 with the assistance of John McGillen, a young altar boy, whose primarily liturgical function that day was constantly sweeping the snow from the altar. Parishioners sat on rough hewn boards held upright by nail kegs and remained bundled in their winter overcoats throughout the service.

From these humble beginnings however the parish grew quickly. The temporary church was dedicated on April 30, 1876 and the school completed and opened on August 27, 1883. The new school, staffed by the Sisters of Charity of the Blessed Virgin Mary, enrolled students as fast as they could make room for them. In fact, in just a few short years a new school was built and dedicated on August 15, 1891. Additional classroom space was still needed almost instantly and was added to accommodate the endless numbers of new parishoners The church too had been outgrown and the cornerstone for the present permanent church was laid on May 19, 1895. The first mass was the mournful Requim Mass for Father Smith who died on September 26, 1896. The formal dedication of the new church took place May 1, 1897.

Within a year, the educational needs of the community again necessitated another expansion, this time to a college which opened as St. Vincent's College (later DePaul University) in September 1898. It too grew rapidly adding a summer term in 1911 and a University Extension program the same year. The youngest parishoners also saw their needs attended to by the addition of the DePaul Day Nursery in 1915.

Today both the parish and the DePaul University flourish on Chicago's near north side. The church stands out as a magnificent Romanesque edifice, flanked by the customary twin bell towers with three levels of narrow, arched windows on all four sides, admitting narrow bands of soft daylight. A magnificent triple concentric circular window crowns the entranceway and permits light to be reflected up the center aisle and bathe the main altar. A small, pointed turret tower highlights the right side of the church front. Side windows throughout are mosaic with top circular design ornamentation but again admitting filtered light to give the interior a sense of regal peace. The strong, bold lines of the exterior echo the depth of the congregation's faith and overwhelming support through the years.

The magnificent twin bell towers of St. Vincent de Paul.

The stained glass side windows with decorative ornamentation and cut molding highlight the workmanship, strength of style and boldness of St. Vincent de Paul Church.

St. Procopius
18th and Allport Street, Chicago, Illinois

Bohemian (Czech) immigrants arrived in the near south side neighborhoods of Chicago shortly after the Civil War. By 1875, their request for a parish convinced the Archdiocese of Chicago to separate the Pilsen area from Sacred Heart and form the new St. Procopius parish. The parish started with the modest purchase of three city lots at 18th and Allport Streets for $3,600, and a Methodist church from 19th and Halsted which was moved to the new site. On April 16, 1876, Easter mass was celebrated in this Methodist-turned-Catholic church for the first time by Father William Coka, who had come to St. Procopoius from St. John Nepomucene, another Chicago Bohemian parish. Within a year, he was joined by the first of three generations of Czech organists and teachers, John Petru, who created the choirs that took the hearts of the Chicago Archdiocese by storm. Their reputation for beautiful Gregorian chants and homeland religious songs carried St. Procopius' reputation far and wide. Likewise, John's functioning as the parish teacher began a solid reputation in educational excellence that saw enrollment grow to 193 students by the end of the first year of operation. With this growth however brought the urgent need for expansion.

Hence, on August 31, 1881 the Bohemian paper *Svornost* announced the plans for a new permanent church, built solidly and to the highest standards of workmanship. By July 23, 1882 the generosity of the Bohemian parishioners enabled the cornerstone to be laid for the Paul Huber designed Romanesque brick church which sported a magnificent bell tower, six stories high, a stone accented front entranceway, a front edifice of four stories, the second of which contains two matching circular windows, the third story three elongated windows crowned by a single four pane circular window and the fourth story has two side by side windows with narrow, elongated windows—all of which reflect light inward and down the center aisle. The bell tower is balanced on the opposite side by a matching four story tower minus the steeple. The perfect symmetry is a tribute to the early workers whose pride crafted this labor of their devotion.

After Archbishop Feehan dedicated St. Procopius on September 23, 1883, the old frame church was converted to the enlarged school and, within two years, eight hundred students were enrolled. This year also saw the Benedictines assume control of the parish with Fr. Neponucene Jaeger as the first Benedictine pastor. Within a few short years a boy's high school was added and St. Procopius College founded. 1892 was another momentus year for St. Procopius for it was now the largest Bohemian parish in the United States. Enrollment in the parish schools reached 1000 children and the beautiful church spire was completed. But growth was not yet at an end. In 1908 the 2000 families of the parish hosted Archbishop Quigley who dedicated the new Lourdes Chapel and surrounding garden where the faithful gathered in large numbers to pray for assistance and to worship at the shrine. An additional eleven lots were purchased in 1912 for a children's playground (now paved). With these additions, St. Procopius became the neighborhood gathering spot for the children who were to become the mainstay of the church, as they entered the priesthood, raised families and future students, and gave to the support and maintenance of the church. This became particularly important as more of the earlier founders moved to the western suburbs to newer and more vibrant Bohemian neighborhoods. And yet even this did not stop the building and parish growth.

In 1953 the old school was completely gutted and remodeled using the plans of architect William Sevic. The same year a new brick convent was completed for the Sisters of the Third Order of St. Francis who staffed the school. These new buildings continued to serve the changing parish as it transformed itself from Bohemian to Hispanic in character and enrollment. Important changes were incorporated to recognize this new ethnicity. A Spanish language mass was added by the bilingual Benedictines and Our Lady of Gaudeloupe was incorporated into the south wall of the Lourdes chapel. The old Romanesque church however continued to serve as the spiritual home of these new immigrants and illustrated a familiar trend in the history of Chicago Catholicism, where one nationality built a church to reflect the homeland of its origin—usually magnificent and representing the highest workmanship possible—and then over the years adopted new nationalities, new immigrants, and new patron saints. But the magnificent early church remained—sturdy, proud and useful—as a symbol of the new congregation's equal devotion which matched the early fervent power of its builders and was now responsible for its maintenance and continuance.

The magnificent front facade of St. Procopius shows the Romanesque artchitecture highlighted by the balanced side towers and soaring spire.

The top of the spire of St. Procopius appears to disappear into the sky with only the top cross appearing to signal its uppermost point.

Our Lady of Guadeloupe on the south wall of the Chapel of Lourdes of St. Procopius parish. The beautiful cut stone serve as a magnificent white background for the inset shrine.

The beautiful statue of Mary atop the tower of the Lourdes Chapel at St. Procopius.
Mary is standing atop the world with hands outstretched in welcome.

St. Paul's
2127 W. 22nd Place, Chicago, Illinois

The lure of steady employment at the McCormick Works (later known as the International Harvester plant) brought a new wave of immigrants, principally German, to the growing south side of Chicago. Sensing that this was to be a neighborhood of growth, Father Emmerich Weber, a native German and the first pastor, acquired a small cottage and stable in 1876 and began outfitting them as a combination church and school, a common practice at the time. Within three years, a large frame building formerly owned by St. Francis of Assisi parish, was moved to the site, placed on a new brick foundation, and enlarged. A four room temporary school was built in 1881 and a permanent school, designed by Schracks and Ottenheimer, was built in 1892. When it opened, the *Inter Ocean* paper reported that: "The streets and houses for blocks around were gaily decorated with flags and streamers, and many of the houses were festooned with evergreens and flowers. Flags of all of the kingdoms of the German Empire mingled with the stars and stripes."

With this completed, Father George Heldmann, the new pastor, could turn his attention to the construction of a permanent church. He directed its architect, Henry J. Schlacks, to design a church that would look at home in Germany's Moselle Valley from where a great number of the parishioners could trace their roots. Fr. Heldmann's congregation not only donated their money to the construction but completed much of the work themselves as many were skilled artisans, masons and bricklayers. When completed, St. Paul's was not only the first brick Gothic church in America but it was built without using a single nail. Only brick and steel were used making the church fireproof. When completed the beautiful edifice measured 290 feet in length and 108 feet in width.

The front twin towers, completed in 1900, are each 32 feet square at the base and rise 245 feet high. Originally illuminated crosses topped each bell tower but now solid crosses have taken their place. The entranceway is a three door arched brick and wood door masterpiece with each topped by a circular glass window for reflecting light up the main altar runway. The Gothic roofs of side porticos are a striking balance to the front facade and arched doorways extend around the building. In 1916 a marble floor was added to the interior of the church and in 1922 a pulpit of Carrara marble was completed and installed by the Daprato Statuary Company. That same year Schlacks travelled to Europe to select the mosaic tiles to be used for the facial and figure carvings located throughout the church interior. Choosing the tiles of the Cav. Angelo Gianese & Co. of Venice, Italy, he purchased over 2,500 sq. ft. of mosaics, individually colored glass, the largest no more than one-half inch square. These were then assembled in Italy, shipped to Chicago in 1930, and re-assembled by John Martin. Perhaps the most striking mosaic pictures are those of the twelve apostles and Christ which adorn the communion rail. Twin side altars, designed by Schlacks and executed by McBride Studio in 1926, completed the interior adornments.

When completed, Fr. Schlimm, the new pastor, has succeeded in making the interior of St. Paul's a masterpiece of European religious art transported to America to give the faithful a sense of the grandeur left behind.

Today the parish serves more than the original German founders. Polish and Mexican Catholics have joined the parish and increased the families served by the parish to over 600. Each Sunday they worship in their Gothic "cathedral" built by the sweat of their German forerunners who just wanted to create a masterpiece that reminded them of home.

The beautiful Gothic architecture of St. Paul's, the church built without using a single nail.

This close up of one of the three entranceways to St. Paul's shows the intricate brick work that the German artisans labored so long on.

The interior of St. Paul's shows the beautiful brick work topped by
the intricate mosaics of Christ's life.

Bro. Ron Fialkowski of St. Paul's staff busily prepares the main altar for Sunday services. The Gothic church is massive yet gives the worshipper a sense of awe and pride at the intricate brick work.

St. Gabriel
4522 S. Wallace, Chicago, Ill.

The Canaryville neighborhood of Chicago was attracting hordes of new Irish immigrants in the late 1870s and early 1880s. This enormous influx led the Archdiocese to appoint the Rev. Maurice J. Dorney as its new pastor on April 11, 1880.

By November of the same year, Father Dorney had already begun construction on a combination school and church. The Sisters of Mercy were contracted to run the school which opened in September of 1881. Father Dorney was an activist priest who ardently took up the cause of his flock by finding many of them jobs in the nearby Union Stockyards meat packing plants mediating labor disputes, and trying to keep saloons out of the residential areas of the parish. He earned the affectionate title of "King of the Yards" for his labor and community social crusades.

The temporary church gave way to the new St. Gabriel's on May 27, 1888, when Archbishop Feehan dedicated the present St. Gabriel's Church. Growth in the parish was astronomical. By 1894, 680 children were enrolled in school and by 1895 a high school program was needed. By 1905 it too was opened. Both the elementary and high school were free to parishoners. The generosity of their parents giving to their utmost ability covered educational costs.

Architecturally, St. Gabriel's transports the passerby to a medieval world of splendor. It is of Romanesque design executed by Chicago architects Daniel H. Burnham and John Wellborn Root. This was the only Catholic church ever designed by this prominent duo. The school was designed by William J. Brinkman. The bricks of the church, while now weather-beaten and in dire need of repair, range in color from red to ebony black, bathing the church in gradations of color depth. A square bell tower with round turrets at the four corners reminds the passerby of a medieval castle watch tower. At the base of the tower are three elongated and inclined windows for light reflection. A broad-winged angel stands guard over the tower. The front entranceway consists of three doors with individual arched roofs and a solid stone cross over the center. Above is the characteristic round window of which there are eight small circular panes of glass surrounding a center circular pane which admits a soft light to the front of the main aisle. Small side alcoves today contain not the original statues but cracks, mortar repairs, weather lines and decayed wood embellishments. Inside three marble altars, installed in 1922, call the faithful to worship. Architectural historian J. Carson Webster, when reviewing the church after its 1949 fire and refurbishing, noted, "Despite changes, the building still has a degree of individuality and character recalling the Rookery, by the same architects."

By the 1980s many of the Irish American families began that decade's move to the South and Southwest sides of Chicago and to suburbia. Those that remained were joined by the new immigrants—Italians, Poles and Mexican-Americans. While the Stock Yards are now closed and the congregation is multiethnic, the church still stands as a proud overseer of the spiritual vibrancy of Chicago Catholicism.

St. Gabriel's is a splendid example of the only Romanesque church design by Chicago architects Daniel H. Burnham and John Wellborn Root.

A statue alcove of St. Gabriel's is empty, deteriorating, and a victim of the
elements----not like the support of its parishoners.

The Statue of St. Gabriel, namesake and protector of the church, in front of brick stairs carved into the side of the building and ascending towards heaven.

The intricate carved motifs of St. Gabriel vividly display the ravages of time.

St. Alphonsus
1429 W. Wellington, Chicago, Illinois

By the early 1880s, a large influx of German immigrants crowded into the apartments and tenements of the Lake View section of Chicago. The immigrants, ethnically conscious of, and strongly protective of, their ethnicity and faith, persuaded the Rev. Joseph Essing, pastor of St. Michael's to purchase land so that the mission church of St. Alphonsus could construct an outstanding tribute to their heritage and faith. Thus, on January 22, 1882, five acres of land was purchased for $9,000 from the Union Mutual Life Insurance Company and immediately thereafter a wooden frame combination church and school were begun. By October 8, 1882 the almost nonstop construction produced the first St. Alphonsus. It was dedicated by Archbishop Feehan, along with the new school which was staffed by the School Sisters of Notre Dame of Milwaukee, Wisconsin. Enrollment at the new school reached 200 by the end of the 1882-1883 school year.

Almost immediately however the flood of immigrants outgrew the temporary church. The new pastor, Father Henry Schagemann of the Redemptionist fathers, began planning for a new, larger and permanent church. Sufficient funds were quickly gathered from the dedicated parishoners and the cornerstone for the imposing new Gothic "cathedral-like" church was laid on September 22, 1889. Adam Boos and Josef Boettinghofer began the initial planning which was ably extended and executed by the architectural firm of Schrader and Conradi of St. Louis, Missouri. The lower church, or more popularly known as St. Gerard's chapel, was completed by March 1890. On October 3, 1897 the completed St. Alphonsus was dedicated.

But this was to be only the beginning for St. Alphonsus. The next several decades were to see increased growth and absorption of newly arriving parishioners, the opening of a two year commercial high school in 1897, the completion of a new brick school, and the addition of a new rectory and convent in 1928. By 1933 over 1,800 children attended the parish school. Growth continued unabated and then tragedy struck. In October 1950, St. Alphonsus was gutted by a massive fire which was to do $600,000 in damage. The interior of the church sustained almost total devastation but the exterior remained strong and viable. Within two years the devotion and generosity of the faithful enabled the renovation to be completed to its old glory. Furthermore, this generosity was no longer obtained solely from the original German church members. American Indians, African-Americans, Filipinos, the Irish, Italians, Slovaks, Spanish and Vietnamese immigrants from virtually every corner of the globe pitched in their meager resources. St. Alphonsus had become one of the most ethnically diverse parishes in Chicago.

Today, the lovely Gothic church stands as a beautiful reminder of the workmanship and grandeur of the German founders. The front facade consists of a striking central entrance flanked by identical, but smaller, side entrances all displaying painted roofs, arched door molding, carved wooden doors, and fine stained glass accent panels. The central clock tower rises majestically and is a crowning jewel of the stonecutters art, with eight windows, carved and symmetrical molding for the borders, a clock where the hours are marked by Roman numerals, and a spire with double rows of corner spires topped by crosses. Four smaller corner spires, carved in a modified papal tiara design, balance the spires of the clock tower extending upward from St. Gerard's chapel. The hours of artistic workmanship, the grace of design, and the attention to detail provide the new parishioners of St. Alphonsus with a glimpse into the talents and pride of the charter members of the congregation as they designed and built a church that reminded them of the Rhine and Ruhr Valleys of their fatherland. Today, all ethinic groups call the church their home and participate in a myriad of church-sponsored activities.

The Gothic splendor of St. Alphonsus highlights the workmanship of German stonecutters, artisans and designers. The clock tower, set off by corner spires, rises majestically upward.

The clock tower of St. Alphonsus is a marvel of workmanship which sets the clock in a sea of carved moldings, arches, and windows to demonstrate the pride of the German founders.

The side entrance to St. Alphonsus accentuate the carved stair posts, the arched windows and the fine craftsmanship of the German artisans.

St. Laurence
7140 S. Dorchester, Chicago, Illinois

It was 1883. The southern boundary of Chicago did not yet extend past 39th Street and Hyde Park was an autonomous town rather than a Chicago neighborhood. Prairies, fields of flowers and native grasses, and level expanses of marshland characterized the Parkside neighborhood where originally vegetable gardens outnumbered people. The growing Catholic presence however and the rapid building in this area soon signaled a need that could not be fulfilled by the itinerant priest from nearby St. Thomas parish. In fact, when Father William Horan of St. Thomas visited it was a long ordeal but uncharacteristically consisting of a hike along a railroad track, skating across icy ponds in the winter, or simply walking along a beaten path where paved roads were still a future dream.

But here lived a growing Irish Catholic flock with names like O'Brine, O'Donnell, Donohue and Murphy and served by priests with the names Moloney, Horan and Fagan. A temporary church under the direction of Pastor John J. Carroll was called for and subsequently authorized for the corner of 76th Street & Kenwood Avenue, the first church in what is now called the Grand Crossing District. In 1889, the Archdiocese gave its new pastor, Rev. Sylvester Moloney, permission for a parish hall to be built and finally in 1890 sanctioned the purchase of a church site at 73rd Street & Madison Avenue (now Dorchester). The present site was obtained in 1901 when 250 feet of land was added to the parish holdings. The always present Catholic school was staffed by the Sisters of Charity of the Blessed Virgin Mary of Dubuque, Iowa who energetically educated the children who were to be the future leaders of Chicago. The Sisters of St. Dominic from Adrian, Michigan assumed school control in 1913.

St. Laurence saw its vast interior finally decorated in a style befitting the faith of its founders when in 1927 the Rev. Denis J. Tuohy retained Professor Gonippi Raggi, a graduate of Rome's St. Luke's Royal Academy of Fine Arts, to complete the church decoration. He immediately began a series of paintings of ecclesiastical events and personages, installed stain glass windows crafted in the studios of Emil Frei of Munich, added three marble altars, and electrified the church's fixtures. Truly now its interior beauty matched its imposing exterior.

St. Laurence endures today, a marvelous spired brick building with a triple front entrance, ascending stone stairs, and glass windows stained in striking patterns on its facade to pour the day's light directly up the main aisle. The Irish donors of this working class neighborhood wished to build a church that would last for generations so that their children's children could remain anchored to their neighborhood and their faith—a common article of faith that was not to be completely abandoned even though neighborhoods changed, populations shifted, and children dispersed.

St. Laurence Church sports a solid brick bell tower with ornamental turret. The belfry is attached to the main church and surpasses it in height, drawing attention to its melodious calling of the faithful to prayer.

The belfry of St. Laurence Church. Note the step brick design, the use of bricks for the crosses on each corner, and the pillar and arches of the tower windows.

St. Cecilia's
45th Place Between Wentworth and South Wells, Chicago, Illinois

The year was 1885. South side parishes like St. Gabriel's and St. Ann's were overcrowded and still the housing increased, the immigrants arrived, and the children needed to be educated. To relieve the pressure on the established parishes, the Rev. Edward A. Kelly organized St. Cecilia's. A temporary structure was erected on 45TH Place between Wentworth and South Wells Sts. For four years this small church ministered to the ever-increasing residential Irish community while money and final church authorization were gathered for the erection of a permanent site. On September 15, 1889 that dream came to fruition with the laying of the cornerstone of a stately Romanesque church layed out by the Most Rev. Patrick A. Feehan. By 1891, the magnificent brick church, modeled after the central portion of the Church of Notre Dame in Paris, with its famous pipe organ began pouring forth the Ave Maria as passersby could hear the beautiful melodies as they walked past the open church doors at 6 A.M. on their way to work. If they would have stepped inside the octagon edifice, they would have stood stricken by the 150 foot high ceiling and the forty feet wide sides designed by New York architect I.B. Bourgeois.

So successful was the church that a brick rectory was added in 1901 and the much needed school appended the same year. The school was staffed by the Sisters of Mercy and within a few years enrolled 750 students, attesting to the enormous Catholic migration to the south side during this and subsequent decades.

Unfortunately, St. Cecilia's did not survive. After decades of growth and stability, working class Catholics began deserting this area for the newly established south suburbs. Considerable racial change also occurred with non-Catholic African-Americans moving into all sections of the parish. As the photos on the following pages attest, the wrecking ball destroyed not only a church and its magnificent pipe organ but an architectural centerpiece of the community. Thus, on November 19, 1972 the final mass was said at St. Cecilia's and in January 1973, the beautiful old church came down, replaced by a vacant lot strewn with urban litter. St. Cecilia's became a parish past but a memory much savored.

A January 1973 photograph of the front entranceway to the Romanesque church with a portion of the altar visible. A remnant of the discarded pipe organ lays to the left, no longer capable of leading the faithful in hymns of rejoicing and praise.

A masterpiece of Romanesque architecture, St. Cecilia's meets the wrecker's ball in January, 1973. The simplicity of external brick design, the curved archways, and the straight lines evoked a common elegance now lost to the ages.

Before its demolition, St. Cecilia's, on 55th Place between Wentworth and South Wells,
combined the look of a Roman stadium and a medieval castle in its sturdy
character and simple strength of design.

A side view of St. Cecilia's
door almost gives the viewer a
sense of looking at the
entranceway to the Colisseum.
Shortly after this photo was
taken the demolition was complete.

The remnants of the beautiful pipe organ lay near the entrance to St. Cecilia's during demolition. Not even this piece of musical splendor was saved to be given to another church. The destruction was complete.

The simple side entrance and marble steps stoically admitted the faithful of St. Cecilia's.

Saint Leo
78th & Emerald, Chicago, Ill.

The Auburn Park neighborhood of Chicago was growing by leaps and bounds in 1885. St. Anne's Parish was overflowing with new immigrants and simultaneously growing past its capacity to minister to the faithful. A new parish was needed and Father P.M. Flanagan of St. Anne's searched until he found a public school at 81st and Wallace that permitted him to begin saying mass for those parishioners further south of his church. By 1886 growth again necessitated expansion and Father Carroll of St. Thomas Parish in Hyde Park arranged for a wood frame mission building to be constructed at 79th and Normal. Until 1896, this mission served as the new parish of St. Leo's.

It was not long however before the need for larger seating capacity forced Father P. Egan, the pastor, to construct a large frame church at 78th & Emerald Ave. The parish was thus established as a permanent entity due to the burgeoning population and in 1905 the Archdiocese was propelled to approve the construction of a beautiful Italian Lombardy style church with a seating capacity of 825. The former temporary structure was converted to the parish school, staffed by the Sisters of Providence, and opened its doors to the children of its parishioners. The parish continued thriving and prospering, only interrupted in its march to success by a substantial fire on October 19, 1914, which caused extensive damage to the church necessitating a complete interior renovation, the installation of a new organ, and the replacement of interior pews, windows, and religious artifacts. The repairs were completed in 1916 with the generous assistance of the church community and St. Leo stands today as a bastion of architectural splendor on the near South Side.

St. Leo's magnificent Italian Lombardy architecture appears as elegant today as it was in 1905.
Note the twin towers, unmatched in size and style on the top, but congruent beneath.

Overhead and to the right of the front entrance of St. Leo's is this ornate carving of the angelic child, enveloped in angel's wings, and watching over those who enter.

An excellent example of the intricate workmanship of St. Leo's, crafted by artisans who took pride in their craft and wished to extol their religion to the neighborhood through their artistry.

Our Lady of Mt. Carmel Church
630 W. Belmont Ave., Chicago, Ill.

Our Lady of Mt. Carmel, founded by Archbishop Feehan in July of 1886, was, at the time, the only English speaking church between St. Vincent's on the South and St. Mary's of Evanston on the North. This must have made the Rev. Patrick O'Brien, the first pastor, feel both unique and challenged as he began planning his new temporary church for the corner of Wellington Ave., and Blucher Sts. By 1888 the ever needed school, under the direction of Sister Mary Catherine Feehan of the Sisters of Mercy, was opened and immediately attracted the sons and daughters of the Irish faithful. Setting up the parish in what would today be considered frontier conditions where living arrangements were sparse and fund raising a constant strain, took a toll on Father O'Brien and he died in 1895, being replaced by Father Patrick Gill. Father Gill oversaw the construction of the new permanent church—a magnificent English Gothic building with twin quad level towers providing balance and majesty to the three arched windows at the main entrance. The almost universal heavy cross flanked by miniature spires rise toward the heavens. Three wonderful stained glass windows over the entranceway filter the morning light into green, blue and gold reflections of the church's glory. The intricate carvings, iron grating, and apostolic crowns bedecking the side porticos lend an elegant English cathedral grace to the stately design, which is followed through in the adjacent Carmel Prayer Center. Here the Virgin Mary stands guard over the three steps rising as an entrance ornament, almost as if beckoning the faithful to rise to heaven to greet her. This Gothic grandeur stands proudly today as a reminder of the glory days of Chicago Catholicism when workers put their souls as well as their pocketbooks into their work.

The Carmel Prayer Center of Our Lady of Mt. Carmel carries on the Gothic strength of design and three step door crowning so indicative of the main church.

The side entranceway of Our Lady of Mt. Carmel with the ecclesiastical coat of arms, intricate wrought iron, and four spire matching design to the front entrance.

The magnificent front entrance with the twin towers flanking plain but strong Gothic architecture at Our Lady of Mt. Carmel.

St. Martin's
59th St. & Princeton Avenue, Chicago, Ill.

In July 1886, the Rev. John M. Schaefers was appointed the first pastor of the new St. Martin's to be located at 59th Street and Princeton Avenue. Almost immediately, a 50 x 90 foot combined church and school building (and an adjacent rectory) was begun. By 1895, as was so common during this heyday of Irish and German immigration, the growth of the parish soon outstripped the small building's ability to serve its parishioners. The principally German congregation saw the need to request a permanent structure from the Archdiocese. Approval was swift and the construction of the wonderful German Gothic cathedral-like building began in earnest. The parish expended the then fantastic sum of $200,000 for the construction of the church, designed by Henry J. Schlacks, and the remodeling of the old combination building into a free standing school. A rectory and convent were added and by 1895 construction was completed.

The embellishment of the church was truly a labor of love. Four large bells were cast for the ornate spire, imported carved wooden stations of the cross in individual window niches were lovingly put in place, light pyramids and votive altars for statues were placed around the interior church perimeter, hand hewn and carved pews were set in place, confessionals were intricately carved wooden symbols of German craftsmanship, and Munich stained glass windows and Innsbruck studios were strategically placed throughout to reflect the exterior light through a cascade of blended color and heavenly scenes. A grand organ of seventy-two registers completed the opulence of the church interior. In 1908 dollars over $60,000 was spent making the furnishings of this parish one of the richest of its day.

Within a decade the enormous construction debt and interest had been retired by the 500 families in the parish—a generosity enormous even for that time. The church prospered for decades afterwards, the school, under the Franciscan Sisters of Milwaukee, enrolled over 500 students, and the faithful came on Sundays to enjoy the marvel their sacrifice had built on the land soon to abut the Dan Ryan Expressway.

As befell so many parishes in Chicago however the neighborhood changed, the German background retreated to the suburbs, and the new residents were not primarily Catholic. By the 1980s the church began to deteriorate, repairs went unfunded, and the number of parish families declined. In the early 1990s the Archdiocese made the decision to close St. Martin's and subsequently sold the beautiful old church to a Protestant denomination. What remains today are the memories of that past grandeur and the following photographs show the depth of affection those early German families felt for their church.

A magnificent recessed alcove carving of Christ as the Shepherd. These ringed St. Martin's telling a story of faith to those who entered.

St. Martin's church stands as a Gothic German masterpiece on Chicago's south side.

The stunning stained glass with the mosaic effect above the altar of St. Martin's.

The magnificent stained glass windows and painted icons of St. Martin's ceiling as they captured the day's light.

A magnificent carved wooden confessional of St. Martin's.

The main altar of St. Martin's. Note the intricate carved wooden spires rising from the altar, reminiscent of the exterior copper spires pointing heavenward.

One of the
recessed stations
of the cross at
St. Martin's.

A breath taking marble statue of the Virgin Mary cradling Jesus after his crucifixion.

The front entranceway of St. Martin's
as it beckons the faithful to
Sunday services.

The golden statue of St. Martin which
could be seen soaring above the Chicago
skyline as it protected its Church and stood
as a beacon for all to see and come.

The magnificent
spire of St. Martin's
in green copper
and slate shingle
towering over
Chicago's southeast side.

A chilling carving depicting a fallen angel clinging to the exterior of St. Martin's.

St. Joseph
4821 S. Hermitage, Chicago, Ill.

Another of the Union Stock Yards parishes in the Town of Lake, now Chicago's south side, St. Joseph's was founded to serve Polish immigrants who toiled in the meat packing plants. As the number of new immigrants was far outstripping the ability of St. Mary of Perpetual Help, the nearest Polish parish, to care for their spiritual needs, in 1885 the Archdiocese directed property to be purchased for the new church. A small mission church was thus begun and dedicated on December 19, 1886 with Rev. Stanislaus Nawrocki as its first pastor.

As was the usual pattern during the immigrant waves of the last decade of the 19th Century, this temporary mission church proved inadequate. Thus, in 1895, the new pastor Rev. Michael Pyplacz contracted with Polish architect T. Lewandowski to design a new brick church, which was dedicated on October 6, 1895. An early press release which appeared in the *Inter Ocean* newspaper described the new church as, "One of the finest on the south side... 162 by 77 feet. It will be of stone and pressed brick, and will cost $90,000. A steeple 175 feet high will ornament the front of the church." It took approximately three years for the beautiful church and attendant school to be completed.

By 1903, rapid parish growth necessitated an addition to this church and school (which boasted 710 students) served by the Sisters of St. Francis. But it too rapidly proved to be insufficient for the ballooning Polish population. By 1913 the new pastor, Father Stanislaus Cholewinski, broke ground for the permanent new church which was dedicated by Bishop Rhode on August 10, 1913. The cost for this new Romanesque landmark was $200,000, paid for by the generosity of its parish's faithful. St. Joseph's, however, gave back to the community in an equally generous way—organizing a day care facility, assisting in the settlement of new Polish workers desperately in need of jobs and housing, opening a free medical clinic and a residence for working girls. These institutions flourished over the next several decades as did the school population. By 1937, thirty Felician nuns taught 1424 children. Over the next several decades repairs were made to the aging buildings, additional social services were provided, and the church took on its present role as neighbor servant for a dedicated congregation.

St. Joseph's has the characteristic two Romanesque bell towers, highlighted by ornately carved trim, arches and moldings. Three arched entranceway doors are bordered by twin pillars and topped with stained glass. A huge frontal facade glass circular window consists of sixteen individual circular panes bordering an interior glass design of eight tear drop panes enveloping a singular four leafed glass pane. Atop is a wonderful statue of St. Joseph holding the Christ child, who in turn is holding the world in his hands. The front entrance is lit by a beautiful globe of five separate lights with a flower design base and an ornate four arm design. The classic beauty reveals the depth of feeling held by the founding immigrants and sustained by today's parishioners.

St. Joseph's on 48th and Hermitage is an exquisite example of Romanesque architecture
with two ornately carved bell towers.

The statue of St. Joseph holding the Christ child with the world in his hands. Note the ornately carved niche molding and twin pillars flanking the statue cubicle.

St. Joseph's is lit at the front entrance by this beautiful five globe electric lamps with four individual arms and carved leaf base.

St. Hedwig
Webster and Hoyne Avenues, Chicago, Illinois

The year was 1888 and the growing Polish community of Chicago's northwest side was expanding so rapidly that a fourth Polish parish was needed. The Archdiocese again asked the Resurrectionist priests to form the parish. Immediately, plans were drawn up for a combination church and school (a common practice in the decades 1870-1920), to be built on property purchased the previous year by the Rev. Vincent Barzynski. Fr. Vincent's brother Joseph was chosen as the first pastor. Within a year the new St. Hedwig was ready to be dedicated and on December 4, 1888 Archbishop Patrick Feehan performed the honors. The school portion of the new building was staffed by the Sisters of the Holy Family of Nazareth.

The church and school were finished with little time to spare, for within five years over 1,300 families were being served by the new church. But then a major controversy temporarily forced the closing of St. Hedwig in early 1895. A siftine of historical fact, and some conjecture, led to the conclusion that Fr. Anthony Kozlowski, a recent immigrant and the new assistant pastor, had dreams of assuming the pastorship of the parish and had no desire to wait years for Father Barzynski to move on. Therefore, he fomented an internal controversy to convince the Archbishop that he would be the more efficient administrator of the parish. When the Archdiocese instead appointed the Rev. Joseph Gieburowski as the new pastor, rumor has it that he instigated a rather large crowd of Polish women to storm the church rectory in protest. Archbishop Feehan could no longer tolerate the dissension and temporarily closed the church. It did not reopen until approximately three weeks later. When it did on February 25, 1895 a new pastor, the Rev. Eugene Sedlaczek, was named the pastor. Fr. Kozlolwski did not surrender so easy however. He obtained a court order halting the proposed changes, celebrated mass in a rented store, and served as spiritual leader of a substantial dissident faction of the parish. St. Hedwig's however was finally reopened on June 23, 1895 with still another new pastor, the Rev. Eugene Piechowski. While the Archdiocese prayed for unity, Fr. Kozlowski promoted further schism by organizing a new parish, All Saints. Archbishop Feehan could take the insubordination no longer and excommunicated the rebellious priest on September 29, 1895. Rather than knuckle under to church authority, Fr. Kozlowski led about 1,000 families to his new parish, founded a splinter sect, the Polish Old Catholic Church, and in 1897 became one of its bishops. To this day, All Saints remains the headquarters of the Polish National Church in Chicago.

Meanwhile Father Piechowski, the new pastor, set about rebuilding the decimated parish. This Polish born priest worked tirelessly toward that end and by the turn of the century so many families had returned to St. Hedwig that the old church and school were overcrowded. Obtaining permission to resume construction on the new permanent St. Hedwig's was obtained and the present church was dedicated on October 27, 1901. By now 4,000 people were in the parish and 800 children in the school.

Father Piechowski succeeded in making St. Hedwig's a true neighborhood landmark. Its beautiful solid stone and brick construction is strong and simple yet contains enough ornamentation (along with its rounded twin bell towers, center cupola and front column construction) to demonstrate the love of the artisans who built it. Wonderful examples of this craftsmanship are evident on the three arched windows on the second story front facade. Twin columns support the roof entablature which contains a border architrave using sets of three columns as the repeating design. Each column is topped by decorative capitals in a peeled back leaf design. Even the surrounding building shrubbery today lends a rustic, peaceful look to a church which was beset by so many feuds in its infancy.

Once completed, St. Hedwig's continued to grow. By 1921 a three story school annex had been completed at the then amazing cost of $160,000. By 1925 it was jammed with 2,651 children and 39 nuns, all eagerly learning catechism as well as English, mathematics and social studies. But this was not an end to the growth. Near the end of the severe depression years (1937), a new convent designed by Leo Strelka was completed. Simultaneously, repairs to the aging building were completed and new furnishings brought the interior up to modern standards. Membership now reached an all time high of 3,000 families.

But as happened to so many of Chicago's immigrant parishes profound change was to radically alter the parish. In 1960 the new John F. Kennedy Expressway was opened. The land acquisition and route of the new road divided the parish in two, forced many families to seek new homes, and precipitated a drastic decline in the parish school enrollment. Virtually overnight the number of children in classes dropped to 700. The second wave of change came in a new ethnic group joining the parish. As Polish families relocated new Hispanic immigrants took their place and the first Spanish language mass was celebrated on December 14, 1969. The challenge of this new ethnic mix has however been successfully met by St. Hedwig and the parish continues to thrive today. The stately old church is still a masterpiece of architecture, a peaceful oasis for the neighborhood and a strong reminder that ethnic compositions may change but old buildings continue to accommodate, the bells merely toll a different tune and the doors welcome different immigrants.

The twin bell towers of St. Hedwig with their majestic rounded domes are balanced by the center cupola of matching columnar design.

The windows of St. Hedwig display a remarkable tri-column motif on the architrave and wonderful capital ornamentation.

The cornerstone of St. Hedwig was laid in 1899 by Archbishop Feehan.

A small window of St. Hedwig's clearly displays the pride of workmanship that arranged the cut stone in a sunburst pattern for dramatic effect.

St. Viator
4160 W. Addison Street, Chicago, Illinois

Eight families and twenty-five square miles of land was the territory allotted to the new parish of St. Viator in 1888. It was to this band of widely dispersed Catholics, and the prospect of future growth, that the Archdiocese of Chicago made a commitment, the foresight of which was to prove prophetic for eventually twenty-five parishes would be carved out of the original boundaries of St. Viator. The new parish was staffed by the clerics of St. Viator with Father Cyril Fournier C.S.V. as its first pastor. Growth at first was slow but steady for the small frame church originally located at Belmont and Pulaski. The majority of new Catholics arriving on the northwest side of Chicago however were settling far north of this site and in 1904 the new pastor, Rev. T. J. McCormick gained Archdiocesan approval to move the church to Addison and Kedvale. Growth then began to accelerate, requiring a new brick combination church and school. Designed by architect William F. Gubbins, the second St. Viator's was dedicated on June 26, 1910. The school continued to be staffed by the Sisters of St. Joseph of Carondolet, Missouri. By 1916 a high school was needed for the expanding enrollment and it continued to operate for eight years until Alvernia High School was completed.

By the beginning of the 1920s, the pastor, Fr. James Ryan, requested Archdiocesan approval to build the present permanent church complex. As new Catholic families began pouring into the northwest side of Chicago, purchasing new single family bungalows on tree-lined streets and rented apartments in well kept buildings, the old church and school combination could no longer accommodate the 1,000 families and 800 children being served. Fr. Ryan received his approval and pledges of support by parishoners poured in when they saw the plans for the beautiful new Gothic Tudor church and cloister that was to be the pride of their neighborhood. And the plans were extensive and ornate. There were to be twin spires with a tiara effect for the pinnacles, a triple door entranceway and carvings reminiscent of the great cathedrals of Europe. So generous was the congregation that the cornerstone was ready to be laid on November 13, 1927. The total projected cost of $300,000 bespoke the magnificence that was to come. When it was finally dedicated on May 5, 1929 by Cardinal Mundelein, the new church complex also contained a new rectory, an almost completed new convent, and interior decorations that were chosen with an eye for the greater glorification of God. The school too was beginning to get overcrowded and, due to depression constraints, even the chapel was pressed into service for additional classrooms. But even these lean years did not halt donations and the parish continued to prosper throughout the New Deal and World War II.

By the beginning of the 1950s another school addition was needed. The parish also decided to build a recreation center for the youngsters of the parish and, again exemplifying the generosity of the parishoners, it took only a single afternoon of door-to-door campaigning to raise the necessary funds. By August 1958 the new recreation center designed by Barry and Kay was a reality and the leisure hours of the parish youth were provided for. Again the parish proved farsighted for membership reached 1700 families by 1980 and continues to serve second and third generation Polish families with a new mix of Filipinos, Hispanics and Puerto Rican immigrants. But, as with so many other parishes, the old characteristics have not substantially changed. The new immigrants work together to meet the financial obligations of the parish to the best of their ability and the pride in their church remains as fervent as before.

St. Viator is a beautiful example of Gothic Tudor architecture accented by twin frontal spires and a triple door entrance.

St. Viator's is decorated with meticulously carved heads, flowers and mythical figures.

A side entrance of St. Viator displays matching twin spires to the front entrance, lancet arches, and intricate ornamentation.

Even the door lighting of St. Viator's is ornate as are the massive wooden and glass door panels.

Part II

Immigrant Migration and Ethnic Diversity
Come to Chicago: 1890-1910

"Streams of population coming from
many sources will make great people."

----*Patrick A. Feehan, Archbishop of Chicago*

St. Maurice
3615 S. Hoyne, Chicago, Illinois

The Bridgeport neighborhood of Chicago is probably most widely known as the birthplace of Chicago's mayors. But in the 1890s, it was also the area where German Catholics were migrating in order to be close to available jobs in the Union Stock Yards and furniture and iron works plants and outlets in the area. As their numbers increased so did the desire to create a new parish which would serve their needs and remind them of home. The Archdiocese listened and the Rev. John Genuit was named the new parish's first pastor, celebrating his first mass in the new $6,000 two story church building on October 12, 1890. Barely was this temporary structure complete than plans were made for a larger combination church and school, which was completed at a record pace, being dedicated by Archbishop Feehan on July 10, 1892. The school, under the direction of the Sisters of St. Francis, enrolled 52 students their first year and 150 by the third year.

By the end of World War I, the new pastor, Father John A. Neumann, saw his parish lose the exclusive German character and gain a diverse group of Polish, Irish, English speaking and Italian immigrants. While the ethnic mix of the parish changed, the growth remained unabated so that by the mid-1930s the pastor, Fr. George J. Wunder, received permission to build the present St. Maurice's church. Ground was broken and the cornerstone laid on July 12, 1936. Fr. Wunder had retained the architectural firm of McCarthy, Smith & Eppig to design a Gothic brick church that would reflect the German heritage of the parish founders. One of the most distinctive features of the new church, built at a cost of $150,000, was an imposing clock tower whose massive Roman numerals struck the hours with German accuracy. The clock tower spires, now green copper with aging, reach up to a cross which presides over the neighborhood as a haven of refuge. The double center carved wooden doorway is crowned by a large arched window, ornamented with decorative lattice work and containing a beautiful array of multi-colored stained glass panes which create a myriad of colored luminescence down the center aisle. The brick work and strength of design certainly exemplify the German heritage of the early immigrants.

St. Maurice's was dedicated on June 13, 1937 by Cardinal George Mundelein. Through the subsequent years the parish changed in ethnicity, so that now Polish and Hispanic parishioners comprise the majority of the congregation. But as residents have moved, some things have remained the same. The clock still keeps perfect time, the brick still exudes a quiet strength of purpose, and the stained glass still lifts the hearts and lights the way for the faithful.

The Gothic brick of St. Maurice's beams out a solid strength of German construction so prevalent in the homeland of the first parishioners.

The beautiful clock tower of St. Maurice with Roman numerals that have assisted the neighborhood in telling the correct time for the past six decades.

Sts. Cyril and Methodius
5009 S. Hermitage Ave., Chicago, Ill.

The Union Stock Yards on Chicago's south side attracted immigrants from many European backgrounds, each tending to form a parish that paid particular attention to their needs and preserved their ethnicity. For the Bohemians that new parish was to be Sts. Cyril and Methodius. Their new parish began on November 14, 1891 when the first pastor, Thomas J. Bobal, himself a Moravian, purchased ten lots at 50th and Page (now Hermitage) Sts., at the bargain price of $5,250. Construction began on the temporary frame church on June 10, 1892 and was completed in two months. *The New World* on October 9, 1892 noted, at the church's dedication, that: "The church is...36 X 70 feet with an addition 24 X 32 feet and a school room which will accommodate 160 pupils...and cost about $6,000." The 242 children enrolled were taught by the Sisters of St. Francis of Mary Immaculate from Joliet, Illinois.

This school, and the new permanent church, were designed by Joseph Molitor, although some early church records list his name as Joseph Milton. But as was customary in the high immigration decades of 1870-1920, the hordes of new parishioners demanded a building of greater size and a school of more room. They were thus asked for their generous contributions to build a church which would be the pride of their neighborhood. Their gifts flowed immediately and substantially for by October 12, 1913 Archbishop James Quigley was dedicating the beautiful new Corinthian style church that could accommodate 960 people in comfortable wooden pews.

The church is constructed using Corinthian columns in honor of Sts. Cyril and Methodius' home town of Thessalonica, Greece. The front three door entrance is crowned by four of these huge columns, each dividing a section which contains an upper window of beautiful stained glass with a semicircular top and a small semicircular window below which doubles as a door top to admit light and round off the symmetry of design. A much longer half window with a compatible semicircular design in the apex of the exterior front facade and a solid stone cross atop the front peak.

After World War II school enrollments were boosted by returning GIs and new neighborhood residents. Contributions to the church maintained themselves at a generous pace and became more necessary after a 1958 fire seriously damaged the church sacrisy and sanctuary. The stoic Bohemians however were undaunted. They gave more of their money and time to renovate the church, add a Greek cross to the sanctuary, and install a new tabernacle made by Edward Dorencz and James Pacovsky. Upon completion Sts. Cyril and Methodius, the pride of Bohemian Catholics, looked more beautiful than before—their columns and stained glass setting it apart as the pride of their cultural heritage.

But almost upon the completion of the renovation, the community changed. Student enrollment declined eventually forcing the school's closing in 1980. The parish now serves a diverse ethnic mix, principally African American, and is struggling for survival. Sadly, its beautiful columns are now marked with gang graffiti, much of the stained glass has been replaced, and the needed repairs are being postponed.

Note the intricate carvings on the Corinthian columns of Sts. Cyril and Methodius,
a crowning achievement of Bohemian artisans.

St. Andrew's Church
3546 N. Paulina, Chicago, Illinois

Organized on October 12, 1896, the first pastor, Rev. A. Croke, followed the precedent of so many of his predecessors, i.e. he constructed a temporary frame church to accommodate the charter parishioners and almost immediately began the planning for a permanent structure. Bishop Feehan, seeing the swelling number of immigrants flooding the area of Addison and Paulina Streets, agreed with Father Croke and authorized the preliminary work for a new, permanent church.

With the generous contributions of the families moving into the new parish, the cornerstone could be laid by June of 1912. The ever-present school, built shortly after the parish was organized, was staffed by the Sisters of Providence of St. Mary of the Woods, Indiana. It quickly became a premier educational institution in the area, attracting new students almost weekly, and necessitating the addition of more nuns and classrooms. By the 1920s, the school boasted over 650 students.

While the parish is no longer experiencing this phenomenal growth, its Mission style of Architecture still speaks today of its early mission for area Catholics. Today, amidst the hustle of a crowded urban neighborhood, it stands as if in reverence of its humble beginnings. The church exhibits three pillars crowned with marble carvings and sculptured head protectors at the double front entrance. Above is a large, round center window beneath which are two windows (and one above) to increase the admitted light and filter it to every nave, aisle, altar, bema and apse of the building. Twin side towers flank the front entrance with the traditional bell towers and narrow, round topped, windows for balance and a sense of ascendance prominent in the lines. Each bell tower has a railing and balcony extension near the summit and lovely carved molding supporting the individual tower roofs crowned with crosses. Its strength of form and character have saved its original "mission purpose" with distinction and dignity through the subsequent decades.

St. Andrew's Church, a lovely example of Mission architecture and covered entranceway statues.

The twin bell towers of St. Andrew's with their intricate carved faux balconies and ornate roof moldings.

St. Mary of the Angels Church
1825 N. Wood Street, Chicago, Illinois

By 1897, Irish and Italian immigrants to Chicago were joined by a new nationality—the Polish. Eventually Polish immigrants would make Chicago the second largest Polish city outside of Warsaw. This new wave of immigrants was intensely Catholic and yearned to have their own place of worship. Thus, Archbishop P.A. Feehan gave permission for St. Mary of the Angels to be organized on November 22, 1897 and appointed Father Francis Gordon, C.R., (a Polish Resurrection order), as the first pastor. Father Gordon wasted no time. Land was purchased for the church on January 18, 1899 and by July 2nd of that year the cornerstone of the first St. Mary's was laid. It seemed overnight that workers began construction of the Romanesque tribute to Mary. It was to be a grand church, 230 feet long and 125 feet wide. With it began the school, staffed by the Sisters of the Congregation of the Resurrection, and adjacent halls to serve the children of families with names like Jankowski, Borucki and Sadowski.

It was only a short time however when even this church became too small. Permission for a new, larger church was obtained from the Archdiocese on August 11, 1911. Immediately the faithful contributed what they could to their new home. They succeeded remarkably. Built over a nine year period at a cost of $400,000, today St. Mary of the Angels is a masterpiece of Polish Renaissance beauty with a soaring dome to rival St. Peter's, an entranceway of eight white stone columns supporting a semi-circular glass ornamental window crowned by the apostolic tiara, two cherubs with angelic faces, and three rows of tiles and scroll work forming a protective shell for those entering below. The brickwork over the main entrance is set to resemble mosaic tiles adding to the Roman features. Strength and simplicity of design characterize both the church and the twin towers resembling a castle lookout and both are accented by tall, narrow windows one could easily mistake for gun turrets of a medieval lord's manor. A side cupola and dome show signs of deterioration but remain stately in their beauty and gleaming whiteness while forming a steady and sure presence of strength for the faithful. The workmen of the early 20th Century left a lasting tribute to this northwest side expression of their faithful generosity and later generations did not permit its demise. When decades of decay left this Bucktown "cathedral" in sad need of repairs, today's faithful raised huge sums, completed the repairs, and by 1992 again enabled the church to open its doors to its loyal flock.

The main facade and entranceway of St. Mary of the Angels shows the unmistakable Romanesque features and strength of line.

The stunning crown of the front entranceway to St. Mary of the Angels.
Note the finely sculptured cherubs and papal tiara.

The side dome and cupola of St. Mary of the Angels enveloped in a brick and marble back drop highlighting Romanesque sturdiness.

St. Mary of the Lake
4200 N. Sheridan Rd., Chicago, Ill.

In the last decade of the 19th Century, Chicago began spreading north into the territory then known as Buena Park. Archbishop Feehan, recognizing the need to serve a population that consisted of sixty Catholic families but would soon contain many new immigrants, envisioned a small communiy church of multiethnic complexion exemplified by its ability to unite the diversity of Catholics in the area. He persuaded Henry John Schlacks, a Chicago native to design the church, and appointed the Rev. J.J. Dennison as its first pastor. Within a year the small congregation had raised over $11,000 (the church cost $8,000 and an additional $2,000 for furnishings) and construction began in earnest. This was an enormous sum of money from such a small and working class congregation. But they were undaunted and many of the sixty families appeared for the ground breaking on November 2, 1901. Within just three months, and through a bitter winter, the church slowly rose on land purchased from Mr. Adam Schneider. On February 2, 1902, the first mass was celebrated in the new building and the joyful congregation intoned a beautiful solemn "Oremus" in thanks for their success.

St. Mary of the Lake was built in the Romanesque style, in simple but strong lines, crowned with a four tier bell tower with cast bells on the third tier, and a circular stained glass sculptured entranceway which admitted a soft light which drifted up the center aisle to create a sense of peace and harmony.

Within a short time the architect Joseph W. McCarthy of New York was putting the final touches on the parish school, a a two story brick building with six classrooms, noted in its day for the abundance of natural light admitted and its calmness of interior gray design. The auditorium seated close to seven hundred, contained a built in stage, and was fireproofed—a lesson learned from the Great Fire of 1871. The education of the community's children was entrusted to the Sisters of Mercy of St. Xavier's who immediately embarked on their mission of making St. Mary's a preeminent educational bastion. For its day, the school not only achieved educational prominence, but was known for the "latest" in ventilation, heat, lighting and sanitation, characteristics that certainly contributed to the enjoyment of its students.

The parish has grown through subsequent decades and today still educates its children, now composed largely of one of Chicago's newest immigrant groups, Hispanics. The parish and school under the Rev. Robert Mair however have not lost sight of their mission to preach and teach to the highest ideal within a community of caring helpers.

The strong architectural style stressing strength and functionality characterize
St. Mary of the Lake Church.

The four-tiered bell tower which calls the faithful to services at St. Mary of the Lake
and which leans ever so slightly as it performs its duty.

Epiphany Church
2524 S. Keeler, Chicago, Illinois

As the 20th Century dawned, Irish and German immigrants began to move further west from the city into a pocket bordered by the Burlington and Belt Line Railroad and the drainage canal, now known as South Lawndale. In February of 1901, Father Lawrence A. Erhard was given permission to found a mission church in this area—the future Epiphany. He designed the new combination church and school himself but always with an eye for purchasing a permanent site. This temporary church and school, only one story in height, was ready for occupancy in June of 1902, allowing Sunday services to move out of the former dry goods store that was being used. At this time the parish was still small and remote, but that was to be only temporary for the new Western Electric plant at 22nd St. and Cicero Ave., was completed in 1903, acting as a magnet for working families. And new families came, enough so that by 1910 a three story brick combination church and school was dedicated. The school was staffed by the Dominican Sisters of Sinsinawa and rapidly grew in students so that by 1916, 425 children attended even though only 250 families were in the parish. The wonderful reputation of the school drew many students from other parishes further increasing the enrollment and reputation. The school continued to grow as the ethnic mix of the parish changed in the 1920s to Bohemian and Polish. Many of these new immigrants were Catholic and many were converted through the efforts of the new pastor, Father Matthew A. Cummings.

By 1953 however the old Epiphany Church was too small and in need of repair. Now Msgr. Cummings contracted with the architectural firm of Edward J. Sculte to design the current church, a beautiful lannon stone structure in a modified Byzantine style. Twin stone towers flank the double door entranceway that gives the viewer the feeling of entering a castle with the rising eleven stairs passing over a missing moat. The bell towers each contain long, narrow windows in the medieval castle design for soldiers to fire on the approaching enemy. The arched entranceway of carved stone extends half the height of the bell towers and is topped by a connected eight arched walkway with strong, forceful carvings. The church interior walls were entirely done in sandstone from St. Meinrad Abbey in Indiana. Tall narrow five paned stained glass windows surround the main altar and intricately carved backdrops and cast a multi-colored hue. The church design is substantial and neat, yet ornamented and Eastern in its decoration, reflecting both the style of its founders and the beauty added by later parishioners.

The church, thus finished, was dedicated by Cardinal Stritch on May 30, 1953. From then until now the faith of the parishioners has remained steady although the ethnic mix has again changed. Older Polish and Bohemian families have been joined by newly arrived Latino and African-American families. But all have maintained an active number of church societies, community activities, and respect for the traditions that built this immigrant parish.

Epiphany church has two magnificent bell towers and a double door entranceway that gives the appearance of entering a medieval castle.

The interior of Epiphany church shows the massive sandstone walls and the beautiful
altar back carvings and stained glass windows.

The center statue overlooking the church entranceway of Epiphany Church highlights the strength of design and the creative use of arches in carved stone.

St. Benedict Church
2215 W. Irving, Chicago, Illinois

German immigration into the area known as West Lake View increased dramatically at the turn of the 20th Century. St. Matthias parish on Ainslie and Claremont could no longer serve the burgeoning population of new area residents and its pastor, the Rev. Christian A. Danz, began the talks that were to quickly lead the Archdiocese to approve the new parish. By February 2, 1902, Fr. Danz was able to celebrate his first mass at St. Benedict's new frame church and school combination. Shortly thereafter, the Rev. Joseph Zimmermann was appointed the first permanent pastor. The new school was staffed by the School Sisters of St. Francis and boasted an initial enrollment of 85 students, a figure that within five years was to reach 300.

Within three years rapid parish growth demanded, as was so often the case with immigrant parishes, the construction of a new church and school. The April 22, 1905 edition of *The New World* announced the construction of a beautiful new brick combination church and school (this building is currently Our Lady's Chapel). But with an increase in parish families to 800 by the beginning of World War I, Father Zimmermann was faced with yet another expansion. The old frame school was outmoded and overcrowded. The church could not hold the faithful even after the addition of more Sunday masses.

Thus in 1916 the Rev. Zimmermann commissioned architect Hermann J. Gaul to design a new church. It was to be, in the words of *The New World* of May 29, 1927: "A magnificent church of Roman architecture, a modern up to date school, a large auditorium with meeting rooms and club facilities...It would take nearly $1,000,000 to duplicate these buildings." The age of the million dollar church had arrived and the German parishioners gave freely to make their church a sterling example for their community. They could not complete the church however without the addition of some significant homeland contribution. This appeared in the form of six newly cast bells, the work of H. Humpert of Brilon, Germany. These were blessed by Bishop Edward F. Hoban on March 22, 1926 and tolled their soft melodies as other new additions were unveiled—a new organ, magnificent stained glass windows and hand carved stations of the cross. These were not to be the last additions however. In 1938 the firm of John Cangelosi was hired to completely redecorate the church and Our Lady's Chapel. Plans were also immediately made for the inclusion of a high school, which was completed six years later. The next five years saw the high school grow by leaps and bounds, reaching 553 students by 1925.

After the Vietnam War drew to a close, widespread immigration patterns altered the traditional German domination of the parish. New Latino parishioners soon joined the parish to give the church a high degree of ethnic diversity. These new immigrants quickly grew to appreciate the splendor of their place of worship and its school and have become the guiding members of the current parish councils.

St. Benedict's church is a wonderful example of Romanesque architecture highlighted by an eight level bell tower housing the Humpert bells and a precision clock. Its pillars, nooks, and arched windows bespeak an elegance and dedication reminiscent of the German cathedrals of the 17th and 18th centuries. The front entranceway is crowned by an intricate carving of St. Benedict flanked by German farm scenes and bordered by stone carvings of the Roman banded fasces design. The crest of the front facade is carved to resemble pillars supporting the roof by individual decorative arches. The beautiful pillared design is carried forth in a twin turreted side entrance where again the pillars appear to support the roof. The details of the carvings, the time of execution, and the massiveness of scale point to a congregation proud of its religion and heritage.

The Romanesque beauty of St. Benedict's is highlighted by the eight tiered bell tower containing six Humpert Bells from Brilon, Germany.

The entranceway to St. Benedict's reveals the small pillars which appear to be supporting the roof, the intricate carvings of St. Benedict and German farm scenes, and the imported stained glass windows.

The side towers of St. Benedict's showcase the small, intricate pillars which appear
to be supporting the roofs.

Assumption Church
2424 S. California Ave., Chicago, Illinois

At the turn of the 20th Century, Slovakian Catholics were moving into the near and southwest sides of the old borders of Chicago, the area now just north and west of the Cook County Criminal Courts building on 26th and California. Assumption, the second oldest Slovak parish in Chicago, has never been a wealthy parish except in the devotion of its parishioners. That devotion and a desire to have a church for their own, led the Archdiocese to appoint the Rev. Peter P. Klois as the first resident pastor in 1903. Father Klois only served the parish for five years when, upon his death, the Benedictine Priests of St. Procopious administered to the growing Slovak community until a new, permanent pastor, the Rev. Andrew Marecak, was appointed in 1913. Father Marecak immediately began working with the parish organizations like the Sokols and the Ladies Slovak Catholic Association to raise funds for the construction of a combination church and school so that the faithful could have a building to be proud of, to worship in, and to be a neighborhood solace in hard times.

Enough funds being raised by almost nonstop activities, the new cornerstone of the combination church and school was laid on July 12, 1914. The new building was to be a two story, brick design, a modified Romanesque facade, with a beautiful set of wood and glass double entrance doors covered with a semicircular arch of wood and stained glass depicting a crucifix with ornamental designs and carved moldings. The glass of the front doors has etched crosses which admit the morning light in a heavenly cross of color. The roof is composed of individual tiles topped by a six window cupola. Inside the church's old pipe organ still sends a beautiful air through its pipe and into the audience.

The school of Assumption parish was opened in September, 1914 by the Slovak Sisters of SS. Cyril and Methodius from Danville, Pennsylvania. So the students could constantly be reminded of the Assumption, a beautiful shrine entitled, "Mary Assumed Into Heaven," was built in the parish garden in 1916. By 1919 however, the church and school needed to rely on divine intervention as their heavy debt continued to mount. Only a vigorous campaign to raise donations by the new pastor Fr. Joseph Ronzik halted foreclosure and allowed the church to stabilize its budget outflow. The school, which had temporarily closed, was reopened by the Sisters of St. Francis of Mary Immaculate of Joliet, Illinois. Through constant vigilance, Father Rondzik and his successors were able to pay the bills and slowly move the church forward. Financial affairs were finally on a sound footing when tragedy struck in 1950. On March 2, a fire swept through the church hall. The devastation required parishioners to again reach deeply into their pockets for repairs. Again their strong faith triumphed. Father Chvojka saw the repairs completed, the debt paid off, and on September 13, 1953 Cardinal Stritch help the struggling parish celebrate its Golden Jubilee.

By the 1960s, the Slovak parishioners were joined by the new parish immigrants, largely Mexican and Puerto Rican. Masses were then celebrated in three languages—English, Slovak and Spanish. Parish membership climbed to 500 families and 150 children attended the school. The parish to this day continues to triumph its bilingual character and has continued poor but stable as a refuge for the faithful in a struggling neighborhood.

The simple strong design of Assumption Church is highlighted by the bell cupola and the stained glass windows.

The prized pipe organ of Assumption Church still emanates a perfect sound throughout the church raising the faithful to hymns of glory.

Victor Ramos, a young Hispanic parishioner of Assumption Church, helps keep the church grounds clean as his way of professing his faith.

Blessed Agnes Church
2651 S. Central Ave ., Chicago , Illinois

At the turn of the 20th Century, the area south of Cermak Road was experiencing the same type of explosive growth that the influx of immigrants looking for the numerous available employment opportunities were bringing to the rest of Chicago. Thus, by 1904 the prairies south of Blessed Sacrament Church were turning into neighborhoods of brick bungalows. Archbishop Quigley appointed the Rev. Francis Vanous as the pastoral shepherd for the new Czechoslovakian community to be known as Blessed Agnes. By June 5 of the same year a small brick church, measuring only 30 x 80 feet, was ready to be dedicated. By the next year, a four room school was opened under the principalship of Marie Svitak. Almost immediately 54 students enrolled. By 1907, enrollment had increased so that all four classrooms were full and an invitation was sent out to the School Sisters of St. Francis of Milwaukee, Wisconsin to staff the school and assist with the church.

By 1926 parish membership had grown to 800 families and the new pastor, Father Innocent Kestl, himself a native Czech, began construction on the present, larger church. He contracted with the architectural firm of Joseph B. Rezny to build a sturdy church which would remind the Czech parishioners of the Renaissance churches of home. The November 21, 1926 issue of *The New World*, stated that the church was, "The pride of pastor and parishoners...of Renaissance style of gray pressed brick and steel. A tower 100 feet high adds dignity to the structure which is of fireproof construction. The church auditorium seats 614, while the choir loft will accommodate 200." The final cost of Blessed Agnes was $129,000.

Blessed Agnes continued to grow. By 1930, it boasted 3,800 residents and 500 school enrollees. However, following World War II, many of the Czech residents, now second and third generation, no longer felt the need to belong to an ethnically homogeneous parish and began following jobs and opportunities to the suburbs. To replace them, Polish and Italian immigrants moved in and later were joined by Hispanics, who now comprise the majority of parishioners. While the ethnicity of the church has changed, the devotion of its congregation remains strong and vibrant.

The church stands as a Renaissance tribute to the new birth of the neighborhood. Its triple front entranceway is capped by an ornately crowned triple mosaic window section beneath a lovely twelve petal glass window, both of which filter light up the main aisle. This reflected light is met by the light from the three stained glass windows behind the main altar, itself a magnificent carved tribute to the creator and so reminiscent of Eastern European churches. The strength, devotion and character of the builders of Blessed Agnes are evident in every one of its intricately carved pillasters, windows, ornaments and statues.

Blessed Agnes is a striking example of Renaissance architecture so prevalent in Eastern Europe.

The priest and altar assistants prepare Blessed Agnes for Easter services. The stained glass windows bathe the church in multicolored light.

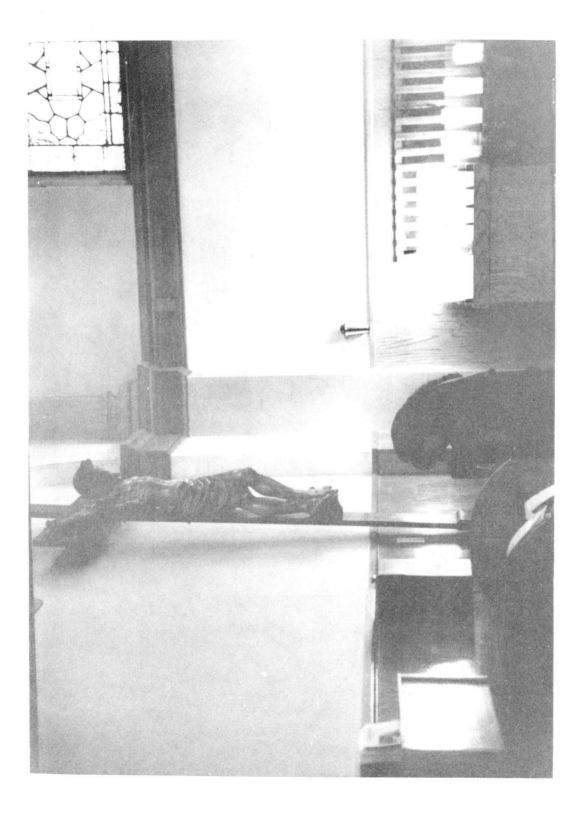

A lone penitent quietly talks to her God at Blessed Agnes church.

The entranceway of Blessed Agnes shows the intricate workmanship of the devoted
Czech founders of this parish.

St. Clement's
642 W. Diversey, Chicago, Illinois

Just west of Lincoln Park on Chicago's near north side the Catholic population was growing by leaps and bounds. By 1905 Archbishop James Quigley felt that neighboring parishes needed relief from their swelling numbers so to keep with the concept of a neighborhood parish that was cohesive, close and a community. Thus, he appointed Msgr. Francis A. Rempe as the first pastor. He immediately began work on a temporary Gothic style church and school that could serve the people while planning commenced for a permanent place of worship.

The parish's first mass thus became a reality on December 25, 1905 and immediately the congregation set about designing their plans for acquiring additional space for a convent (which was ultimately purchased in 1916) and additional funding for a permanent church they wanted to build for the greater glory of God and their faith. While these dreams were in the making practical matters were not forgotten. A school was opened in 1906, staffed by the Franciscan Sisters of Joliet, and immediately began filling its rooms with an ever-growing number of children. The school offered a new feature, uncommon in many parishes, whereby the traditional grammar school was capped by a two year high school with a commercial curriculum.

The present permanent church finally became a reality as construction was completed in 1919 after having taken over two years due to a shortage of manpower and materials occasioned by World War I. When completed, however, its rounded Byzantine dome crowned with a solid rock cross dominated the neighborhood. As had many churches of the time, it sported twin bell towers with long thin double windows and topped by twin pillars in the bell chambers. The tile roof of each bell tower was accented by carved moldings which contained crosses, intricate flower patterns, and a modified egg and dart pattern which showcased the artisan's craft as well as his religion. Side panel carvings are highlighted by an outstanding coat of arms (as illustrated) stressing the virtue of humility and bearing the Latin inscription, "Dominus Adjutor Meus." The attention to detail evident in this insert is characteristic of the exterior adornments and of the faith and effort of the congregation to spare no expense or time on St. Clement's.

St. Clement's Church, a beautiful example of Byzantine architecture, highlighted by the curved dome, heavy stone cross, and twin bell towers.

A side bell tower double pained window which highlights the intricately carved moldings and pillars of St. Clement's.

An example of the beautiful intricate coat of arms carved in a side panel of St. Clement's.

St. John Berchmans
Logan Boulevard and Maplewood Avenues, Chicago, Illinois

St. John Berchmans was organized between the years 1903-1905 by Father John B. DeShryver, S.J. as an immigrant parish for Belgians moving to the northwest side Logan Park area of Chicago. While Belgians represented one of the smaller immigrant communities in Chicago, they were intensely nationalistic and urged that their new parish be organized as a national church. The Archdiocese approved their request and Bishop Peter J. Muldoon laid the cornerstone on August 26, 1906. In January of 1907, Father Julius E. DeVos, a native Belgian, was named as its first pastor. The new combination church and school, located in the church basement, was dedicated by Archbishop Quigley on December 15, 1907 using a three language—English, French and Flemish—ceremony as a sign of respect and solidarity for Chicago's newest national church. The new pastor requested the Sisters of St. Dominic of St. Catherine, Kentucky to provide the instruction for the parish children.

From its very inception St. John Berchmans was a symbol, and the pride of, the Chicago Belgian community. Designed, along with the school, by architect J.G. Steinbach, the magnificent Spanish Romanesque church utilized a triple door entrance of beautiful carved wooden panels surmounted by horseshoe arches, the use of piers to support the lintels, lovely elongated windows with matching horseshoe arches and the lovely use of brick for ornamentation. A wonderful stained glass front edifice window in a flower pattern of eight petals surrounding an inner circle of nine panes rests atop four small stained glass windows with arched designs matching the front facade. The peak of the roof also displays wonderful ornamentation in a candy cane style throughout and topped by a crosslet crucifix. The old wooden front doors still use the hand wrought iron hinges and display a sturdiness so beloved by the early artisans.

St. John Berchmans continued to grow over the next several decades with school enrollment reaching 300 students by 1925. But the student body was now of mixed ethnicity, although Belgians throughout Chicago continued to call it home for holidays and national festivals. This new cosmopolitan character however enabled the parish to thrive, enlarging and remodeling the rectory in 1925 and adding a new convent in 1930. Even in the midst of the depression years the generous parishioners sacrificed much, paying off the church debt, redecorating the church, which now numbered over 3,500 of the faithful, and providing current materials for the 500 children in the school. Likewise, a new sacristy was constructed and the rectory was refurnished to modernize the living quarters of the parish priests. By 1949 a quarter of a million dollars had been raised to enlarge the front of the church and by 1957, with school enrollment peaking at 632 students, ground was broken for a second school of six classrooms at 2508 N. Maplewood. This too was only a part of a continuing parish effort to renovate and redecorate. In the mid-1960s the church interior was refurbished and modernized, a chapel was added next to the sacristy, and the school was modernized. Exterior grounds were carefully landscaped and the church again lost none of its charm but gained a much needed structural face-lift.

It seemed however no sooner had the parish received its new look than ethnic changes in the parish brought on an era of hard times. Many of the old Begian families moved to western and northern suburbs and the new, largely Polish and Hispanic, immigrants did not have the financial ability to sustain the parish in the style to which it had become accustomed. School enrollment dropped to 544 by 1969 and Msgr. Donald J. Masterson, the new pastor and Vice Chancellor, was forced to close the Maplewood school and rent it to the Chicago Board of Education, using the rental income to stabilize the parish budget and offset the rising cost of the remaining school on Logan Boulevard, which now housed all eight grades. A tuition-work school plan, with costs supplemented by several fund raisers, bingo nights and carnivals, has enabled many of the parish children to receive a parochial education. All of these efforts have been successful in making St. John Berchmans the centerpiece of Logan Park activity. Today, the church and school, with their beautiful landscaping, present a quiet picture of old world charm and elegance for the neighborhood. The founding Belgian families built their church but the new immigrants have made it a lasting tribute.

St. John Berchmans is a wonderful example of Spanish Romanesque architecture which provides of the neighborhood a sense of the devotion of its early Belgian founders.

The front facade of St. John Berchmans illustrates the ornateness of the Romanesque architecture, the brick designed horseshoe arches, and the stained glass windows.

The front double wooden doors of St. John Berchmans still utilize the hold crafted iron hinges and give a sense of European castle elegance to the front facade.

St. Kilian
8725 S. May St., Chicago, Illinois

With only twenty-three Irish and German families and a dream, the Rev. John J. Green began St. Kilian's Parish in 1905. His direction from Archbishop Quigley was to provide a well built and glorious church to serve the ever-expanding flood of new immigrant parishioners. To accomplish his purpose, an entire city block was purchased and the plans for an Italian Renaissance style church were drawn up by Joe W. McCarthy. Within a short time Father Green was celebrating mass in the Coronada apartment building, a temporary place of worship. Meanwhile, the cornerstone was laid on September 10, 1905 and the bricks of the new church began ascending ever higher. A new school was also completed in 1915 with a capacity of six hundred students, an estimated need that was to be quickly surpassed. The Dominican Sisters of Adrian, Michigan directed the children's education with a zeal that propelled the school to decades of prominence. As new immigrants continued to enter the parish, purchasing bungalows and brick apartment buildings, a school addition was erected at 8748 S. Aberdeen, adding eight classrooms and boosting capacity to 800 students. By 1927, further increases prompted the Archdiocese to add its first junior high school at St. Killian's. Growth extended well into the 1950s when another five room addition was completed and school enrollment reached 1,195 students. In 1972 the Franciscan Sisters of Milwaukee took control of the school.

St. Killian's was built with the traditional three door entrance topped by stained glass and an inset carving denoting the CHURCH OF ST. KILIAN, using the traditional Latin script. The facade of the church, extending above the doors, contains a large seventy-two pane window with a semicircular top surrounded by arched brick. The window is flanked by two narrow windows of eighteen panes of square stone design. The walls and windows use a Celtic motif in honor of St. Kilian. The interior is bathed in light from the window arrangement and highlights the altar and back plate which contain thirty-seven different types of woods. On the side of the church is a magnificent inset cross formed of the dominant construction brick and containing at the juncture of its arms the carved mystery of the Trinity. In the words of Cardinal Mundelein, "This was truly a sound, substantial edifice."

Today, St. Killian's, under the Rev. Daniel J. Murtaugh, serves a predominately African-American congregation from the Brainard-Gresham area of Chicago. The now closed school has been rented to a nearby Evangelical denomination—a sign of the times where the church, once the dominant spiritual presence of the immigrant neighborhood, now shares its mission with a myriad of competing religions.

St. Kilian's facade showing the strong lines of Roman architecture, highlighted by three raised windows, shining light down the main altar aisle onto the carved wooden altar composed of 37 different types of wood.

The inset cross in the brick facade of St. Kilian's with the mystery of the trinity in the Latin, "PATER, FILIUS, SP(IRIT)US, S(ANT)US EST DEUS and connected by the NON EST (not is) disclaimer." In essence, the motto means that the Father, Son and Holy Spirit are separate but all are God.

St. John of God
1234 W. 52nd Street
Chicago, Illinois

It was 1906, and in the frame and brick bungalows of Chicago's south side (the Sherman Park area then known as the Town of Lake), Polish immigrants were moving in, having taken jobs in the nearby stock yards and heavy industries. This area grew so fast that the Archdiocese quickly named the Rev. John G. Jendrzejek as the first pastor—a hard working priest who quickly gained the hearts of the new immigrants and also lost no time in beginning the new temporary church. He purchased an entire city block, hired the architectural firm of William J. Brinkman, and in April of 1907 began the work on the three story brick building. The cost of Father Jendrzejek's land purchase and the construction of the beautiful church and school was $75,000. Construction moved so swiftly that Archbishop Quigley was able to dedicate the new church by October 27, 1907. Within a year over three hundred families and 360 children were being served by the new parish. Five Felician nuns began the instruction of the children and within a decade twenty-one more nuns were needed to keep up with the enormous growth, which had reached 2,506 students by the year 1922.

The temporary church was likewise soon outgrown and the present church, a beautiful Renaissance, twin-spired building, was begun on October 13, 1918. Work was completed and the first mass celebrated on March 28, 1920. Membership in the parish continued to soar for decades, surpassing the 2,400 families counted in the 1922 census. But as with many parishes in the Back of the Yards area, the inevitable changes to Chicago saw hundreds of families move further south and southeast and to the suburbs. By 1978, only 239 pupils were enrolled in the school and the number of Felician sisters reverted to the original five. While the numbers may have declined, the enthusiasm of the church families has not. They still generously support their church and parish—a fixture of neighborhood pride.

St. John of God's Renaissance edifice is highlighted by twin spires topped by ornate cupolas with hollow, outlined crosses and eight pillars surrounding the belfry. The main entrance contains five entrance doors, evenly spaced, and from which access can be gained by climbing five stairs. The entranceway is crowned by a railing of short pillars beneath a large round window of scalloped glass sections topped with a semicircular roof. The construction attests to the skill of the craftsmen, the sturdy but graceful design of the architects, and the lasting, solid faith of the immigrant builders.

St. John of God is a stately example of Renaissance architecture so beloved by immigrants.
It was designed by the firm of William J. Brinkman.

The beautiful bell tower of St. John of God with the hollow, outlined cross and the pillared belfry.

St. John of God's ornate stone carvings of wreaths, crosses, flowers, scalloped designs attest to the craftsmanship and love of the immigrant builders.

Part III

The Effort to Save One Immigrant Parish----
The Shrine Of The Sacred Heart

Treasure your memories. Let them speak out in your moving along
with the working, day-by-day tasks of justice and truth and
mercy that Church, the People of God, is all about.

----*LaVerne Landon*

Sacred Heart Church
11652 Church Street, Chicago, Illinois

The history of Sacred Heart parish predates its formal Archdiocesan approval in 1892. Rather, it began in 1671 when France claimed the lands abutting the Great Lakes as under their control, and subject to, the French king and the Catholic Church. Almost immediately Catholic missionaries, who hitherto had only traveled with fur trappers and tried to convert local Indians, began establishing missions. One of these first missions was Angel Guardian, founded by Father Francois Pinet, S.J. in 1696 on what is now Chicago's famous Grant Park site. While it only remained opened a few years, this little church, "Built on the bank of a small river," became the earliest predecessor of French Catholic presence in Chicago and began the rapid growth of Catholicism in this area. By 1843, Pope Gregory XVI formally recognized the growth of Catholics south of Chicago by making Chicago its own diocese, no longer subject to St. Louis and appointing Father William J. Quarter its first resident bishop.

While Irish and German immigrants were pouring into what is now central Chicago and also to areas north, west and south of the current downtown, the descendants of the French-Canadians settled in the far south fringes of the city along the old Blue Island Ridge in what is now an area ranging from Alsip to Morgan Park. Many of these French settlers, devoutly Catholic and hard working, bought land, found employment with the Purington Brickyard at ll9th and Vincennes, and began their quest for their own national parish. By 1892, the eighteen families in this remote outpost had secured permission to form Sacred Heart parish on land at 123rd and Rexford in Alsip donated by Mr. and Mrs. William H. Harrison. A nonresident priest traveled to the parish on Sunday by electric train and horse and buggy. This devotion to a church reflecting their ethnicity and their determination to see their religion prosper supported this small frame church until it was destroyed by fire shortly after the turn of the 20th Century. But this tragedy did not deter these devout parishioners. Rather than give up, they began rebuilding their church—but in a new location at 116th and Church Street in Chicago, just north of the Purington Brickyard. Completed in 1904, Sacred Heart was a French national church designed using the baloon frame architecture originally developed by Augustine Dodat Taylor. Built on stilts due to the swampy lowland area, it nevertheless was a graceful and beautiful Greek revival church with white clapboards, a small portico, columns, and a pedimented gable roof. In 1922 the parishoners purchased bricks from the Purington Brickyard to enclose their little frame church, adding a sense of permanence to their shrine. The new enclosed church represented the Mission school of architecture style with the front facade of smooth common brick accented by four semi-circular arched windows. A curvilinear gable roof in front and a pitched roof behind provide a sturdy, simple adornment. Immediately behind the front gable roof is a roof extension, pyramidal in shape, that holds a statue of Jesus Christ with outstretched arms welcoming the faithful to their neighborhood shrine.

SANCTUARY OF THE SACRED HEART, MORGAN PARK, ILL.

An early photograph, pre-1922, of the original frame Sacred Heart Church.
Note the priest standing at the front entrance and the lack of any streets,
paved sidewalks, or huge trees as now adorn the area.

The interior of Sacred Heart at Christmas season.
Note the manger on the side altar and the lavishly decorated main altar.

The interior of Sacred Heart Church shows the intimacy wherein devotions could take place as well as the main altar flanked by two smaller side altars.

With virtually no further interior or exterior modifications, the small church served its faithful, expanded its membership to include many Irish and Germans, and came to represent the pride and devotion of its membership. The faithful service continued until January 21, 1979 when Cardinal John Cody announced the parish would close as repairs were needed and were too extensive and costly and the Archdiocese could not spare a resident priest for the church. While the story of most parishes would end with such a pronouncement, this is only the beginning for Sacred Heart, as its parishioners now were energized to save the church, not only for its historical value but for the miracles supposedly performed there, the attachment to their special church, and the sense of neighborhood that had developed over the years. the fight against Cardinal Cody was on.

The Struggle for Survival

John Cardinal Cody's decision to close Sacred Heart church came as a blow to the thousand plus families who had revered "their shrine" and its history. They were also a determined group of Catholics who wasted no time organizing the "Save Our Shrine Committee" with Thomas Ryan as their president. He immediately set about writing appeals to Rome, Mgr. Jean Jadot, the Apostolic Delegate to the United States, Cardinal Cody, the media and anyone else who would listen. An effort was likewise immediately begun to stress the historical significance of Sacred Heart before Carol Shull of the National Registry of Historic Places and Daniel Kenney of the Illinois Department of Conservation. Much of the historical and emotional significance was directly related to three distinct aspects of the church's history.

The first of these was the "French Connection." Sacred Heart church was the last French mission founded in the United States and was established to serve French Canadians employed by the Purington Brickyards. The first pastor, Father Louis DeMers arrived in July of 1904 from his previous missionary assignment among the Cree Indians of Red Bear Lake, Alberta, Canada. The second area of significance is the attribution of a number of miracles to the veneration of the Sacred Heart which have emanated from the church. In fact, the side walls of the church were adorned with crutches, walking sticks, braces, canes and eyeglasses as well as other remnants of the miracles said to have been brought about in this shrine. Plaques bearing the names of those cured clung to the church rafters as a testimonial to the faith of those who came there and were cured. So great was the number of devotees that in 1922 the Spanish style mission shrine was added on to. In the arched recesses of the brick wings extending outward from the church were added bells which called the faithful to service from the surrounding prairie homes. The interior was redecorated with stained glass windows, paintings and religious statuary. Within this shrine of devotion, Father DeMers dispensed Holy Water and medicine, blessed the sick, and the combination of these three supposedly healed both the bodies and minds of the believers. But perhaps the atmosphere of the shrine also contributed to the healing. Father DeMers was a man in constant motion, animated, jovial and tireless. He might be seen entertaining the faithful with his playing of the pipe organ, his Eskimo huskies, and the homeless dogs who found shelter in his church. The third reason for the preservation of this landmark was the community pride in the little mission church. Homes, stores and boarding houses had grown up around the church and served the almost exclusively French population until 1935 when it became a neighborhood parish church which added Irish and German parishioners to its flock. As a mission having no territorial boundaries, it drew Catholics from near and far into its quaint 35 x 80 foot worship area—an intimate area for communicating with God and asking for his intercession with miracles for the sick and infirm. This devotion formed the essence of the church's service and is what energized the parishioners when the closing was announced.

This 1979 photo of Sacred Heart church shows the Purington brick facade and the intricate and loving care that went into the work.

REV. RAYMOND DE NORUS

Two early photographs of the Rev. Raymond De Norus, a Capuchin Missionary, who was appointed pastor of Sacred Heart in June 1912. He began publishing a small magazine entitled ,"The Blessing," a publication designed to promote knowledge of, and love for, the "Divine Heart of Jesus."

A reproduction of the first page from Father De Norus' writings among the Cree Indians. This would be the ancestor for the "Blessing" he later published at Sacred Heart Shrine.

The Committee To Save Our Shrine

The Committee To Save Our Shrine began its phone and letter writing campaign, sending pleas for help to all who would listen (and some that wouldn't) from the Pope to Mayor Daley. They established a round-the-clock guard for the Shrine, organized sufficient pledges of financial support to insure all necessary repairs would be made, and obtained a promise from a presently unassigned priest to serve the parish. Support rolled in from past and present members of the Sacred Heart community. But from the Archdiocese of Chicago came a disheartening response from Monsignor Bracken who, citing Canon Law on the status of a mission rather than a parish, stated, "You do not seem to understand... there are no parishioners at the Shrine of the Sacred Heart... Hence, we could not respond to parishioners who do not exist." Cardinal Cody's aide had thus expressed the unsympathetic and arrogant aloofness of a Cardinal that the people called "out of touch."

On February 4, 1979 parishioners learned that the Archdiocese had obtained a wrecking permit for the next day. Cardinal Cody was obviously not even going to consider the plea of the faithful. On February 5, 1979, the Committee To Save Our Shrine filed suit in the Cook County Circuit Court seeking an order to halt the demolition until a full hearing could be scheduled on the petitioner's claims. Judge Joseph Wosik, admittedly in unchartered legal waters, issued a 30 day restraining order. Energized, the faithful kept a daily vigil in cold outside weather while they protected their shrine—now already gutted inside by Father Brown, the Archdiocesan administrator, who had stripped the items of value from the church, sold them—pews, statues and stained glass windows alike—to the highest bidder. In the end it was money, not the hearts of the faithful which won the day. Those who had dug deep into their pockets for decades were left with those few artifacts of little value. The past glory and depth of devotion characteristic of the shrine were gone. The faithful no longer believed they counted.

Although it seemed hopeless, the parishioners continued with their lawsuit, meeting again on March 9, 1979 in Judge Wosik's courtroom. The judge urgently requested James Seritella, the attorney for the Archdiocese, to send "someone with authority" to talk to the people of Sacred Heart and report back to court in two weeks. These talks proved fruitless and the Circuit Court regretably denied the petition of the Committee To Save Our Shrine. A ray of hope did occur on June 15, 1979 when Sacred Heart was recognized as an historical landmark by the Illinois Historic Sites Advisory Council. Shortly however this glimmer of salvation was darkened by two developments. On August 17, 1979 the Appellate Court of Illinois likewise declined to intervene on behalf of the parishioners and also prior to the August 31, 1979 deadline, the Archdiocese, as property owner, refused to accept the historical status of the Shrine.

The ordination photo of Father John F. McNally, Pastor of Sacred Heart Church for many
years. Father McNally died Dec. 16, 1963. He was known to his fellow clergy and his
parishioners as a simple priest who dedicated all of his waking hours, and his personal fortune,
to support his church, care for the sick, and help his parishioners with their problems.
He was a "priest's priest." This photo by Laveccha Studios was taken in April, 1928.

But the Committee did not give up. A petition was filed by Sheila Murphy, an attorney for the Save Our Shrine Committee, on January 9, 1980 with the United States Supreme Court for a writ of certiorari, requesting the case be sent to them for full consideration. The Archdiocese, represented by the law firm of Reuben and Proctor, asked the court that the petition be denied. In opposing the request, the Archdiocese used the argument that, "Closing a church is not easy...Unfortunately, Sacred Heart Church is not the first and will not be the last. But the Bishop must provide the maximum pastoral care to the most Catholics...this task is becoming even more difficult as fewer Catholics become priests, resources shrink, and double-digit inflation rages." While this battle raged in the courts, Sacred Heart was added to the National Register of Historic Places and Mayor Jane Byrne of Chicago indicated she would support listing the church as a Chicago Historical Landmark since, she stated, the church could, "Serve as a cornerstone to the community, an inspirational service facility, and a tourist attraction." Her letter, dated March 3, 1980, ironically was delivered the day the U.S. Supreme Court declined to intervene in the controversy.

The cause seemed lost as the Archdiocese decided to reject the parishioner's final requests and reaffirm the closing. Another piece of history had been lost but the controversy nevertheless showed the faith and devotion of those who believed in the Shrine and their duty to try and preserve it. Many of the original documents pertaining to this battle of history and faith versus money and power are included in this chapter so that the reader can truly appreciate the fervor sparked by this debate.

A Letter Written Circa 1908 from the
French Families of Sacred Heart to Chicago's Archbishop

Catholic Archbishop of Chicago
1555 North State Street
Chicago, Illinois

Dear Sir:

We desire to address you respecting Sacred Heart Church at Morgan Park. We, who sign this letter, are all of the French people in the vicinity of this church, and the purpose of this letter is to explain to you the impossibility of our supporting the church alone as we are informed you expect us to do.

Many years ago, when the brick yards at Purington first opened, there were more families, but of late years they have been moving out until they are reduced to us few. The homes of those who moved away are now occupied by Americans and some Irish, but our number is not increasing, in fact, it is decreasing. Our children are brought up as Americans. French is spoken only by a few of those people, and there are only two old ladies who do not understand the English language.

The church, as you know, has a mortgage of $6,000. We have done everything we could (during the past three years the church has been opened) to raise money, but most of the money comes from the Catholics of Morgan Park who are not French. We respectfully suggest that it would be to the benefit of this church, as well as to the community of Morgan Park, if boundary lines dividing the adjoining parishes were drawn. Some of the people at Morgan Park go into the city on the train or by street cars, some go to the church at 99th Street by street car. We cannot afford the expense of railway and carfare, and as the church has been built and as it is in Morgan Park it seems but natural that it should be supported by all of the people of Morgan Park.

If our Village of Morgan Park is to be divided, and this church is left to us to support, you are exacting of us more than we can do, and the church will have to be closed. We dislike to be separated from those who have been with us in this work for the past few years. We have all worked together very nicely, and to us there is no reason why we should have a church by ourselves, especially when there is but a handful of people, earning comparatively small wages, who are out of work quite a period of the year.

Therefore, we write you this letter, asking that you try to view the situation as it is apparent to us, and that you help us keep our church open. You can help us by drawing the division of line between the adjoining parishes, by reason of which the people of our village will all then come to our church. It is in their village, it is near to them, within walking distance for everyone, and we are certain such a division would be acceptable to all.

Very Respectfully,

Peter Boulac

John Martell

Ezra Dion

Mrs. Agnes Lawrence

Frank Benjamin

Narcisse Pare'

Mrs. F. Besoncon

Mrs. L. Lawrence

Mr. Napoleon Benjamin

Mrs. Julia Archambarth

Mr. Moses Clement

Frank Baron

Joe Benjamin

Telesphore Tatro

F. Fredette

A. Castonguay

Sacred Heart Gets a Reprieve

Sacred Heart stood in limbo for several more months until the appointment of Cardinal Joseph Bernadin in 1982 as successor to the late Cardinal Cody. One of the new cardinal's first official acts was to order a review of the case of Sacred Heart and subsequently reverse the official decision to close, and eventually demolish, Sacred Heart. Shortly thereafter, restoration was begun and the small, loved neighborhood church reopened at a mass celebrated by Cardinal Bernadin. Sacred Heart survives to this day fulfilling its original mission of bringing a special feeling of closeness to God to the faithful. The future of Sacred Heart appears secure well into the next century.

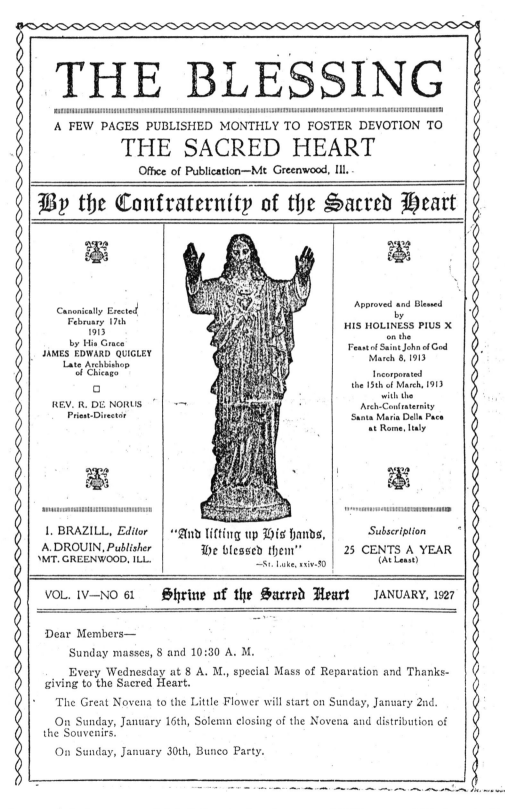

THE BLESSING

A FEW PAGES PUBLISHED MONTHLY TO FOSTER DEVOTION TO

THE SACRED HEART

Office of Publication—Mt Greenwood, Ill.

By the Confraternity of the Sacred Heart

Canonically Erected
February 17th
1913
by His Grace
JAMES EDWARD QUIGLEY
Late Archbishop
of Chicago

REV. R. DE NORUS
Priest-Director

Approved and Blessed
by
HIS HOLINESS PIUS X
on the
Feast of Saint John of God
March 8, 1913

Incorporated
the 15th of March, 1913
with the
Arch-Confraternity
Santa Maria Della Pace
at Rome, Italy

I. BRAZILL, *Editor*
A. DROUIN, *Publisher*
MT. GREENWOOD, ILL.

"And lifting up His hands,
He blessed them"
—St. Luke, xxiv-50

Subscription
25 CENTS A YEAR
(At Least)

VOL. IV—NO 61   Shrine of the Sacred Heart   JANUARY, 1927

Dear Members—

Sunday masses, 8 and 10:30 A. M.

Every Wednesday at 8 A. M., special Mass of Reparation and Thanksgiving to the Sacred Heart.

The Great Novena to the Little Flower will start on Sunday, January 2nd.

On Sunday, January 16th, Solemn closing of the Novena and distribution of the Souvenirs.

On Sunday, January 30th, Bunco Party.

The front page (of six pages which follow) of a January, 1927 copy of Father de Norus'
"The Blessing" magazine published regarding the affairs transpiring at Sacred Heart Church.

THE SACRED HEART OF JESUS

CENTER OF THE LOVE OF CHRIST
By F. R.

The Divine Nature was united not merely to the Soul, but to the Body of Jesus Christ. His Heart is, therefore, a Divine Heart, the Heart of God Himself. To say this is to say all that can be said about the Sacred Heart. It is to place It before us as a Heart of incomparable majesty and greatness, calling for the profoundest homage, love, and veneration we are capable of rendering It.

How sublimely great, therefore, are the treasures that enrich the Sacred Heart! Our mind cannot conceive them, because no mortal mind can grasp the majesty, the purity, the sanctity of God. This Royal Heart is mighty with the strength and majesty of God Himself. This Heart is holy with the holiness of God Himself. This Heart is sweet and generous and lovable and faithful with the sweetness and the generosity, the love and the fidelity of God Himself. O! now, perhaps for the first time, I begin to have some faint idea of the priceless value of the Sacred Heart. O my Divine Saviour! make my wretched heart a little less unworthy of Thee. O Heart of my Redeemer! noble, faithful, generous, and loving, beyond the utmost reach of my imagination, take complete possession of this poor, cold, sinful heart of mine.

What a difference between my heart and that of Christ! Yet all the treasures of His Heart are at my disposal to make up for the almost entire lack of every virtue and good quality that I find within my own. I will borrow of Its sanctity to make up for all my sinfulness. I will clothe myself with Its surpassing strength to fortify my weakness. Its wisdom and Its light shall chase away the darkness of my earthly heart. My heart, so often sorrowful and crushed beneath the trials of this life, shall find a supernatural courage and happiness and peace in Thee, O Sacred Heart of my Redeemer!

In our human way of speaking we attribute to the **heart** the qualities that we admire in the **person**: we say a person is kind-hearted, noble-hearted, generous-hearted, and so on. Of all human passions and emotions that register their workings on the heart of man none affect it so profoundly as does love. Hence in man the heart is taken as the special seat of love. Now Jesus Christ is truly Man, therefore is His Heart the human seat and centre of His love.

Jesus showed His Heart to Blessed Margaret Mary with flames bursting forth from within, to show that His Heart is a very furnace of divine love, the focus of that all-consuming fire of love that motived all His actions from Bethlehem to Calvary, that still keeps Him a willing Victim on our altars and a loving Prisoner in our tabernacles. The secret history of that love is written in His wounded Hands and Feet and Side, and still more in the wondrous mystery of the Eucharist.

And **you have cost that Divine yet Human Heart so many pangs**; you have been the object of Its sweet yet ardent transports. It has thought of you and loved you from the first, and with an intensity of love that neither human lips can tell nor mind conceive. Should you not be His, and His **alone**, for ever more? Should not the one great business of your life, henceforth, be to live for Him and love Him with all the fervour and intensity of your entire being?

The heart is the seat of grief as well as of love—the grief that springs from unrequited love. The Heart of Christ was rent and torn with the unseen martyrdom of love before the soldier's hand had pierced It on the Cross. The fear, the weariness, the sadness that assailed It in the Garden, the awful vision of the sins of men, from which It shrank with such unutterable loathing. Its foreknowledge of the black ingratitude of future ages—all this was Its martyrdom beneath the olives of Gethsemane.

Another martyrdom awaited It within the silent tabernacle. Infinitely and imperturbably happy, yet here, too, in a mysterious manner, that great human Heart of Christ upon the altar, glowing with the ardours of an infinite yet unrequited love of man, waits and longs and mourns for some small recognition of Its love.

And shall not I, at least, endeavour in my own poor way to satisfy the longings of this Heart of love? I have grieved and wounded It in days gone by. With what a wondrous love and patience It has borne with me, waited for me, drawn me back from the abyss! But now and henceforth my one great aim and effort is and ever shall be to make my Benefactor known and loved by men as He deserves, and by my love and service to endeavour to atone in some degree for all the utter coldness and indifference by which my Saviour's Heart is wounded in His own sweet Sacrament of Love.

□ □ □

NOVENA TO THE LITTLE FLOWER

In the joy and excitement of the holiday season do not forget that our annual Novena in honor of St. Therese of the Child Jesus is taking place from January 2 to January 10, with the solemn closing on Sunday, January 16 at 3 in the afternoon. The souvenir for this occasion is something which will be treasured by all who are fortunate in securing one, having been imported from France. Each person attending will be presented with one of these beautiful souvenirs.

HAPPY NEW YEAR

With wishes for a glad New Year,
Repeated oft before,
The dear little "BLESSING" of love
Is calling at your door.

This herald of the Sacred Heart
Brings hope to every breast,
In many a home, from south to north,
From farthest east to west.

This is the wish it bears to you,
Dear reader,—loving friend,
"May love upon your pathway shine,
To light you to the end."

The sacred Love of Jesus' Heart,
That love for ever true;
While to your soul the peace of God
Will come to stay with you.

May every thought and deed of yours,
And every word you say,
All make you draw more close to God,
And happier, day by day.

The little "BLESSING" of Jesus' Love
Is calling at your door,
To wish you Heaven's Eternal Joy,
When Life's brief day is o'er.

□ □ □

VIGIL LIGHT

Have a Vigil Light burned nine days at the shrine for your intention. Offering $1.00.

□ □ □

IN MEMORIAM

Members of the Confraternity and Blessing readers are requested to pray for the repose of the souls of:
Mrs. Alice Walker.
Miss Julia Ryan.
Mr. P. Glennen.
Mr. Thos. Foley.

□ □ □

NOVENA BOOKLETS PUBLISHED AT THE SHRINE

Our Unfailing Petition to St. Joseph.....10c

Our Unfailing Petition to Our Lady of Lourdes (Story of the Apparition)......10c

Our Unfailing Petition to St. Margaret Mary (Story of Her Life).................10c

Our Unfailing Petition to the Sacred Heart and the Promises.................25c

CHATTER BOX

DIAMOND RING

Although December 19 (the date set for the return of the Chance Books has passed) there are still many who have overlooked Father's request that all books on the ring be turned in before Christmas.

□ □ □

If you are one of the many who saw the Eucharistic Congress moving pictures you have probably noticed a banner of the Sacred Heart following the float representing a colossal monstrance. It was the banner of the Shrine carried by the Holy Name men of this parish.

□ □ □

To stimulate and reward the zeal of the Promoters of the Confraternity—Father Ray has decided to call each month at the Confraternity meeting the names of those who have secured at least five new members.

The names called for the month of November are as follows: Mary Moriarty, Josephine Spencer, Loretta Fergny and Elizabeth Corcoran, the number secured this month being 43. members. Remember that Our Lord promised to have engraved in His Heart the name of those who promote this devotion.

□ □ □

A CORRECTION

Our printer made a slight mistake in the December notice of the Novena —substituting the word "Souvenirs" instead of "Services" but we will graciously overlook this small error as it is the first one he has ever made in our many dealings with him.

A MESSAGE FROM FATHER RAY

And now that the year has passed and we are in our first issue of 1927, Father wishes to express his gratitude to the many good friends who have assisted him in various ways during 1926—through that glorious week of the Eucharistic Congress—during the five Novenas — at the monthly Bunco parties and other meetings—to the members of the Raymond Club, the Confraternity Promoters and Members and all the other friends who have helped with their prayers, their labors or their finances he greets you all with a hearty "Thank you and may God bless you through all the years to come."

□ □ □

Father Ray has been the recipient of many beautiful Christmas gifts and he appreciates the thought that prompts the sending of gifts either to the Shrine or to himself personally.

□ □ □

HOLY NAME SOCIETY

Holy Name Society will receive Holy Communion on the Second Sunday of this month.

□ □ □

No. 15—FATHERAY RUBY BRONCHIAL SYRUP

This is with No. 63 our best preparation. A true bronchial syrup. Once tried, always used. Price, 75c, $1.35 and $2.50.

Fatheray Remedies can be had only at the Raynors Pharmacal Co., located in the Postal Telegraph Bldg., 140 W. Van Buren Street, Room 219.

BUNCO PARTY

The prizes donated for November Bunco Party are as follows:

Margaret Burns	1
Loretta Sullivan	4
Mrs. Pauline Connolly	3
Mary Simmons	1
Josephine Spencer	7
Mrs. N. Carroll	1
Mabel McNamara	2
Mrs. M. Bresnaham	2
Mrs. D. Castonguay	1
Margaret Wilson	1
Mrs. Mae Pinkerton	3
Veronica Rodenkirch	1
Anna Rodenkirch	1
Misc.	1
Mrs. Daly	2
Delia Cain	4
Mary Walker	1
Mrs. Rafferty	3
Adelle Jax	1
Mrs. Hunt	1
Mrs. A. Smith	1
Mrs. Wilson	1
Mrs. M. Couture	2
Mrs. M. Reilly	1
Henry Nessinger, Jr.	1
Genevieve Dennis	2
Mrs. T. Fitzgerald	1

☐ ☐ ☐

The electric lamp and luncheon set were won by Mrs. Hunt, 8123 Sangamon Street.

☐ ☐ ☐

Winners of prizes at November Bunco Party:

Mrs. Slattery	Helen McGann
B. Callahan	Mrs. Fitzgerald
Mary Walker	Mrs. Reilly
Mrs. McInerny	Mrs. P. Connolly
M. Schneider	Mrs. McCleary
Mrs. Brick	Gene Dennis
Mrs. Nessinger	Mrs. P. Sablick
Pauline Hall	Eileen O'Connell
Sadie Grimes	T. Hunt
M. Johnski	Mary A. Ryan
Catherine Roberts	Mrs. Downey
Mrs. M. Pinkerton	N. Colburn
Marg. Nessinger	Mrs. Steffen

Mrs. Fashingbauer	K. Keefe
H. Nessinger	Mae Vogt
Mrs. H. Tierney	Mrs. Oldiges
Marie Hall	E. Pfister
Mrs. J. Murphy	M. Verbecker
Miss Lyons	Mrs. Rafferty
Wm. Brick	A. M. Jax
E. P. Steffen	R. Zenkee
M. Whelan	M. Harmon
C. Lyons	Mrs. Ward
Mrs. T. Hunt	R. Franzen

Bunco parties take place on the last Sunday of every month at 3:30.

☐ ☐ ☐

WHAT IS LAUGHTER?

A psychologist tells us that laughter is an expression of emotion, which manifests itself chiefly in certain convulsive and partly involuntary movements of the muscles of breathing. After an intake of breath, the air is expelled from the lungs in a series of successive interrupted, short, abrupt movements of the muscles, respiration accompanied by movements of the face and often of other parts of the body, and the emission of chuckling sounds from the throat. It is generally accompanied by a heightened expression of the eyes which indicates the feeling of merriment, amusement or satisfaction experienced. Sometimes the laughter may be so hard and so prolonged as to produce tears. A smile is a gentle, inaudible form of laughter. It is expressed merely by movements of the lips, face and eyes. It has been said that all unrestrained normal activities of the body give rise to the emotion of joy which is expressed by smiles and laughter. Laughter and smiling are also external manifestations of the play instinct. Laughing is the privilege of man. It is intimately related to the highest intelligence, esthetic and moral development of man. That laughter is most beneficial which laughs with and not at people.

In children, laughter is instinctive, but their expressions of joy usually contain an element of uncontrolled exuberance. Thus, in their pleasure, they clap their hands, stamp their feet and jump about with shouts and laughter in pure excess of vital spirits. How sweet is the sound of childish laughter and how brutal is the mistaken discipline which holds it necessary to suppress the laughter of a child.

Laughter is often an indication of character; it is seldom that two persons laugh exactly alike; laughter ranges from loud explosive shouts to a mere twinkle of the eye; and the study of laughter becomes a study of character. The spontaneous hearty laughter of sincere feeling is very different from the affected and constrained laughter of the pretender. Moreover, there are laughs which betoken peculiar traits of mind and character; laughs that are mechanical or nervous, which express nothing or which mean much; laughs which express good will or guile, friendship or animosity, kindness or cruelty, in fact, as a medium of expression, laughter covers a wide range, indeed.

The secret of success socially, commercially and professionally, lies largely in one's ability to laugh or

smile at the right time and in the right way. A laugh or a smile is pleasing to those who hear and see it. Most of us judge others by what we see, and appearances help to fix our impression of individuals. If we get pleasure from a smiling countenance, we regard its owner with friendliness and respect. Let us then smile to give pleasure to others and gain their friendship. Smile upon others as you would have them smile upon you. Let us pass on the leaven of cheerfulness and good will by "smiling through" in happiness, good health and prosperity on the one hand, and in the face of adversity on the other! Smile, and the world smiles with you.

A smile costs nothing, but gives much. It enriches those who receive, without making poorer those who give. It takes but a moment, but the memory of it sometimes lasts forever. None are so rich or mighty that they can get along without it, and none are so poor but that they can be made rich by it. A smile creates happiness in the home, fosters good will in business, and is the countersign of friendship. It brings rest to the weary, cheer to the discouraged, sunshine to the sad, and it is Nature's best antidote for trouble. Yet it cannot be bought, begged, borrowed or stolen, for it is something that is of no value to anyone until it is given away.

"We have loved him during life; let us not abandon him, until we have conducted him by our prayers into the house of the Lord." St. Ambrose.

"Blessed are they that mourn, for they shall be comforted."
St. Matt. V. 5.

Sweet Jesus have mercy on the soul of

Rev. Raymond de Norus
Died July 20, 1951

GENTLEST Heart of Jesus, ever present in the Blessed Sacrament, ever consumed with burning love for the poor captive souls in Purgatory, have mercy on the soul of Thy servant, bring him far from the shadow of exile to the bright home of Heaven, where we trust, Thou and Thy Blessed Mother, have woven for him a crown of unending bliss. Amen.
May He Rest in Peace. Amen.

Your gentle face and patient smile
With sadness we recall,
You had a kindly word for each
And died beloved by all.

The voice is mute and stilled the heart,
That loved us well and true,
Ah, bitter was the trial to part
From one so good as you.

You are not forgotten loved one
Nor will you ever be
As long as life and memory last
We will remember thee.

We miss you now, our hearts are sore,
As time goes by we miss you more,
Your loving smile, your gentle face
No one can fill your vacant place.

The original mass card at the funeral of the Rev. Raymond de Norus,
July 20, 1951 with his photo shortly before death.

CONFRATERNITY OF THE MOST SACRED HEART OF JESUS.

I consecrate myself to the Most Sacred Heart of Jesus and desire to be enrolled in the Confraternity of the Sacred Heart of Jesus, Morgan Park, Ill.

Name_____

Address _____

City_____

(Detach and mail to Rev. Father Raymond de Norus, Morgan Park, Chicago, Ill.)
[OVER]

A request for subscriptions to the magazine "The Blessing" circa 1930 when the price of the publication was 60¢ per year.

"THE BLESSING"
"The Blessing" is the only magazine of the kind in the language. Its primary object is to honor the Sacred Heart of Jesus and to make Him better known and better loved. It commends itself to all who wish to see the Devotion to the Divine Heart widely extended.

A MONTHLY MAGAZINE
Subscription Price 60c per Year

For all information concerning Masses, Novenas, Registration of Consecration to the Sacred Heart, Membership in the Sodality of Our Lady of Deliverance, Subscription to the "The Blessing," Manual of Devotion to the Sacred Heart, offerings of candles, lamps, flowers, etc., application must be made to
REV. FATHER RAYMOND de NORUS,
MORGAN PARK, ILL.

An original document, dated December 10, 1952 from Chicago's Archbishop Samuel Cardinal Stritch, and signed by him as Bishop of Chicago, entitled "DECRETUM ERECTIONIS CONFRATERNITATIS DOCTRINAE CHRISTIANAE."

*The Sanctuary Guild of
Sacred Heart Church
cordially invites you to attend
a retirement reception given in honor of*

Reverend Kenneth Borchardt

*Sunday, the twenty-fifth of June
nineteen hundred and seventy-eight
two o'clock until six in the evening*

*at Father McNally Hall
Sacred Heart Church
11652 Church Street
Chicago, Illinois*

Fr. Kenneth Borchardt was appointed by Albert Cardinal Meyer as Pastor of Sacred Heart following the death of Father John F. McNally in December, 1963.

A local parishioner guards Sacred Heart Shrine during the days immediately following its closing. Note the beautiful Purington bricks atop the stone foundation.

Sacred Heart adorned with flowers for the first Christmas mass after the church was temporarily reopened. This is the basement of Sacred Heart as the upstairs had been stripped of furnishings.

A Copy of the Original Application (5 Pages) to the
National Register of Historic Places Dated Jan. 4, 1980
and Requesting Sacred Heart Church Be Placed
on the Register for Preservation

FHR-8-300 (11-78)

United States Department of the Interior
Heritage Conservation and Recreation Service

National Register of Historic Places
Inventory—Nomination Form

See Instructions in *How to Complete National Register Forms*
Type all entries—complete applicable sections

For HCRS use only
received JAN 4 1980
date entered JAN 28 198

1. Name

historic   Sacred Heart Mission Church

and/or common   Sacred Heart Church, "Mission du Sacre Coeur"

2. Location

street & number   11652 South Church Street   ___ not for publication

city, town   Chicago   ___ vicinity of   congressional district   2nd

state   IL   code   012   county   Cook   code   031

3. Classification

Category	Ownership	Status	Present Use	
___ district	___ public	___ occupied	___ agriculture	___ museum
X building(s)	X private	X unoccupied	___ commercial	___ park
___ structure	___ both	___ work in progress	___ educational	X private residence
___ site	**Public Acquisition**	**Accessible**	___ entertainment	___ religious
___ object	___ in process	___ yes: restricted	___ government	___ scientific
	___ being considered	___ yes: unrestricted	___ industrial	___ transportation
		___ no	___ military	___ other:

4. Owner of Property

name   Archdiocese of Chicago

street & number   Post Office Box 1979

city, town   Chicago   ___ vicinity of   state   IL   60690

5. Location of Legal Description

courthouse, registry of deeds, etc.   Cook County Recorder of Deeds

street & number   130 North Clark Street

city, town   Chicago   state   IL   60602

6. Representation in Existing Surveys

title   None   has this property been determined elegible? ___ yes   X   no

date   ___ federal ___ state ___ county ___ local

depository for survey records

city, town   state

7. Description

Condition
_____ excellent
_X_ good
_____ fair

_____ deteriorated
_____ ruins
_____ unexposed

Check one
_____ unaltered
_X_ altered

Check one
_X_ original site
_____ moved   date _____

Describe the present and original (if known) physical appearance

Sacred Heart Mission Church is a structure best described as vernacular architecture. It faces east, being 35' wide and just over 80' deep. To the rear on the north side is a short "L" which provides adjoining living quarters. The church is somewhat unusual in that there is no basement. Instead, the ground floor is a community space with ancillary storage and utility rooms, while the main (second) floor is the sanctuary. The basic configuration of the building and the uses of the spaces is as it was when the building was completed in 1904. It has, however, undergone many changes in the 75 years since its dedication.

In 1904 the Sanctuary of the Sacred Heart as it was first called was built in Morgan Park, Illinois, now a Chicago neighborhood. The location was on property donated by William H. Harrison and his wife to the Catholic Bishop of Chicago. The property was of little value, being essentially swampland. The original building was of balloon frame construction, entirely of wood. The façade was apparently Greek Revival with a small portico supported by two columns and a pedimented gable. The windows were four-over-four sash windows; two, on the facade, were topped with semicircular fanlights. There was a bell tower with a pyramidal roof surmounted by a cross on the north side of the building. The building was sheathed with white clapboards. No cost records have been retained, but it is reasonable to assume that the construction budget was quite small.

During the first two decades after construction, little change was made to the structure. However, the congregation made numerous donations including oil paintings, images, statues, carvings, and stained glass windows. In 1922 the congregation, having become more affluent, elected to refine and fireproof their church by converting it to a brick structure. They encased the original building within a veneer of brick walls. No major changes were made to the interior, and the basic proportions of the exterior were not changed. No specific architectural style was adhered to, although it is reminiscent of the Spanish Mission style. Apparently the round-headed windows on the facade provided some sort of inspiration, for all windows were given this treatment in the remodeling. The same motif was used in closing the earlier Greek Revival entry, and at the center of the front cornice. The belltower gained a new, steeper roof with a slight flare, and the cross gave way to a statue (apparently donated by a member of the congregation). Both sides and the rear corners of the building were given brick pilaster buttresses at this time. These were required for structural stability and are aesthetically pleasing. A quasi-mansard roof can be seen at the top of each side wall. Two colors of brick were used, with the darker tone accenting the windows and corners of the building.

The interior of the building has undergone far less alteration than the exterior. It still contains the original handmade black walnut pews. Fourteen stained glass windows remain in the sanctuary. Beautifully made, they show the influence of the Art Nouveau. For many years the church has had a splendid set of the "stations of the cross" adorning its walls along with numerous works of art contributed by the congregation. Many of these have been removed recently but are in storage and will be returned if the building remains standing (one gift to the church, a Mason and Hamlin reed church organ built in the 1880s, will be returned when preservation is assured, for example). Other art objects remain in place. All of these items represent more than 75 years of contributions from an extremely loyal congregation, many of whom are descended from the original members of the church.

8. Significance

Period	Areas of Significance—Check and justify below			
____ prehistoric	____ archeology-prehistoric	____ community planning	____ landscape architecture	x religion
____ 1400–1499	____ archeology-historic	____ conservation	____ law	____ science
____ 1500–1599	____ agriculture	____ economics	____ literature	____ sculpture
____ 1600–1699	____ architecture	____ education	____ military	x social.
____ 1700–1799	____ art	____ engineering	____ music	humanitarian
____ 1800–1899	____ commerce	____ exploration/settlement	____ philosophy	____ theater
x 1900–	____ communications	____ industry	____ politics/government	____ transportation
		____ invention		x other cultural group

Specific dates 1904-1979   **Builder/Architect** Unknown

Statement of Significance (in one paragraph)

During the latter part of the seventeenth century and the early decades of the eighteenth, the French government encouraged missionary activity throughout the Great Lakes and Mississippi Valley areas. Missions at Kaskaskia, Cahokia, Vincennes and (briefly) Chicago became important seats of French culture in the Illinois country, then a part of the province of Quebec. Nor did the cession of Illinois to the English in 1763 put an end to the establishment of French mission churches in Illinois; St. Mary's Mission Church in Chicago, for example, was founded by Father J. M. I. St. Cyr in 1833. It later became a parish church and was destroyed in the Great Fire of 1871. Sacred Heart Mission Church possesses state-wide significance as the last French mission church in Illinois--that is to say, the last founded (1892; existing structure built 1904) and the last closed (1979). It possesses additional local historical significance for its associations with Chicago's French-speaking community.

History

In 1892 the Sacred Heart Mission Church was founded by Father J. A. Milot in Alsip, Illinois (about a mile from what is now the southern boundary of the city of Chicago) to meet the needs of the far Southwest side's growing number of French Canadian immigrants. Many of them worked at the vast Purington Brick Yard in nearby Morgan Park. When this first church building was destroyed by fire, services were in fact held for a time in the brick yard itself. In 1904 the existing structure was built on some nearby swampland donated for that purpose. A cluster of homes, stores, and boardinghouses grew up around the French mission church. And, as paved streets were laid out, it seemed only natural that the lane in front of Sacred Heart should be named "Church Street." A succession of pastors (French missionaries until 1935) not only ministered to the community but taught English and otherwise served the special needs of the immigrants while helping them to become integrated into the larger society around them. Sacred Heart remained a mission church throughout its existence. A mission church--as opposed to a parish church--has no territorial boundaries from which it must draw its congregation. Thus, Sacred Heart continued to serve (until this past year) the descendants of its first members as they prospered and dispersed throughout the metropolitan area.

Sacred Heart Church is one of the few tangible reminders of the French presence in Chicago, despite the city's long association with that people. The very first European settlement there was the Mission of the Guardian Angel, founded by Father Francois Pinet in 1696. Although it was abandoned just four years later, the portage at Chicago remained an important route for fur trappers throughout the eighteenth century (the Chicago Portage National Historic Site was listed on the National Register in 1966). In 1779, Jean Baptiste Pointe du Sable of Haiti became Chicago's first permanent settler (the site of his home was listed on the National Register in 1976). As late as the 1830s a majority of Chicago's

9. Major Bibliographical References

See continuation sheet.

10. Geographical Data

Acreage of nominated property ____Less than one____
Quadrangle name ____Blue Island____   Quadrangle scale ___1:24000___

UMT References

A |1|6| |4|4|1|4|0| |4|6|1|4|6|0| B |_|_| |_|_|_|_|_| |_|_|_|_|_|_|
  Zone   Easting   Northing   Zone   Easting   Northing

C |_|_| |_|_|_|_|_| |_|_|_|_|_|_| D |_|_| |_|_|_|_|_| |_|_|_|_|_|_|

E |_|_| |_|_|_|_|_| |_|_|_|_|_|_| F |_|_| |_|_|_|_|_| |_|_|_|_|_|_|

G |_|_| |_|_|_|_|_| |_|_|_|_|_|_| H |_|_| |_|_|_|_|_| |_|_|_|_|_|_|

Verbal boundary description and justification

Lot 1 in Block 3 in Resub. of Blocks 4 and 11 in Vincennes Road Addition, a sub. of the
W ½ of SE ¼ of Section 19, Township 37 North, Range 14 East of the Third Principal Meridian
in Cook County, Illinois.

List all states and counties for properties overlapping state or county boundaries

state	code	county	code
state	code	county	code

11. Form Prepared By

name/title 1. Mary Olsson, Assistant 2. Jeffrey S. Flemming, National Register Coordinator

organization
1. Beverly Area Planning Association   1. April, 1979
2. Illinois Department of Conservation   date 2. December, 1979

street & number
1. 9730 South Western Avenue   1. 312-233-3100
2. 405 East Washington Street   telephone 2. 217-782-3340

city or town
1. Chicago, Illinois
2. Springfield, Illinois   state

12. State Historic Preservation Officer Certification

The evaluated significance of this property within the state is:

____ national   _X_ state   ____ local

As the designated State Historic Preservation Officer for the National Historic Preservation Act of 1966 (Public Law 89–665), I hereby nominate this property for inclusion in the National Register and certify that it has been evaluated according to the criteria and procedures set forth by the Heritage Conservation and Recreation Service.

State Historic Preservation Officer signature

title   date 12/26/79

For HCRS use only
  X I hereby certify that this property is included in the National Register

                                       date 1-28-80

Keeper of the National Register

Attest: date 1-28-80

FHR-8-300 (11-78)

**United States Department of the Interior
Heritage Conservation and Recreation Service**

National Register of Historic Places
Inventory—Nomination Form

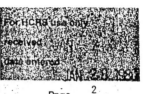

Continuation sheet Sacred Heart, Chicago   Item number   9   Page   2

Clayton, John, The Illinois Fact Book and Historical Almanac, 1673-1968. Carbondale,
            Illinois: Southern Illinois University Press, 1970, pp. 2-4.
Department of Development and Planning, Historic City: The Settlement of Chicago.
            Chicago: 1976.
Garrathan, Gilbert J., The Catholic Church in Chicago. Chicago: Loyola University
            Press, 1921.
Mulligan, Mary, and Bill Nigut, "The People of Sacred Heart vs. the Catholic Archdiocese,"
            Chicagoland Monthly. Chicago: April, 1978.
New Catholic Encyclopedia. New York: McGraw-Hill Book Company, 1967. Vol. IX, pp. 967-71.

The Response of Sheila Murphy, Attorney for the Save Our Church Committee on Why the Church Should be Listed on the National Register of Historical Places

RESPONSE TO COMMENTS MADE BY THE
CATHOLIC BISHOP OF CHICAGO REGARDING
THE LISTING OF SACRED HEART MISSION
CHURCH ON THE NATIONAL REGISTER OF
HISTORICAL PLACES.

(Department of Interior No. 436)

O'DONNELL & MURPHY
55 East Monroe Street
Suite 4005
Chicago, Illinois 60603
(312) 263-5747

TABLE OF CONTENTS

I.

INTRODUCTION
___

Sacred Heart Shrine was listed in the National Register of
Historic Places on January 28, 1980. Subsequently, the Catholic
Bishop of Chicago filed objections. Sacred Heart Shrine was re-
moved on March 19, 1980, due to a procedural error. The Respondent
was given full opportunity to respond by Carol D. Shull, Acting
Keeper of the National Register.[2]

On February 15, 1980, Respondent charged by comments in the
Chicago Catholic,[3] a weekly newspaper, that Federal Code abuse had
occurred by the listing of Sacred Heart Church in the National Register
of Historic Places. The Chicago Catholic has a weekly distribution of
approximately 175,000 readers. However, in an earlier editorial in
the Chicago Catholic on February 8, 1980,[4] the Respondent admits that
Sacred Heart Shrine was historically designed to serve French-Speaking
Catholics. Sadly, the Respondent accuses the National Register of
Historic Places of falling victim to "political manipulation"...
and "attempting to make history serve politics".

This newspaper, the mouthpiece of Respondent, regrettably,
cruelly criticized members of the United States Senate and members of
the House of Representatives for performing the duties they were
elected and sworn to perform.

1. Hereinafter referred to as "Respondent".
2. Petitioner's Exhibit No. "1".
3. Petitioner's Exhibit No. "2".
4. Petitioner's Exhibit No. "3".

On February 15, 1980, James A. Serritella, Attorney for the Respondent, had a letter written to the National Register published in the _Chicago Catholic_.

Certainly Respondent can use his newspaper to express his point of view. However, it is unseemly for the Respondent to criticize other United States citizens in the exercise of their own First Amendment rights. Respondent filed formal objections on April 18, 1980, to the placement of Sacred Heart Mission Church on the National Register of Historic Places. Petitioner will respond _in seriatim_ to the points raised by Respondent.

Petitioner is joined by the Department of Conservation for the State of Illinois in their request that Sacred Heart Mission Church be again and _finally_ placed on the National Register of Historic Places.

II.

ISSUE

—

Respondent cites cases in his comments that are entirely irrelevant to the issue at hand.

The issue is quite simply:

<u>Do citizens have the right to have Sacred Heart Mission Church placed on the National Register of Historic Places</u> without interference from the Roman Catholic Church?

Emphatically, the answer is yes. Indeed, Respondent concedes this issue in favor of Petitioner.[5]

The listing of Sacred Heart Mission Church does not require the church to be operated as a church; Respondent can administer his archdioscese without any governmental inference.

How sad that Respondent does not glory in the nomination of Sacred Heart Mission Church as countless other bishops have done! The French influence in America is part of the firm foundation of our country.

No one is suggesting here that Respondent should be compelled to operate Sacred Heart Mission as a church.

Respondent states that he owns the building that..."once housed Sacred Heart Church." Respondent alleges that Sacred Heart Mission is no no longer a church,[6] therefore, the National Register of Historic Places should be permitted to place Sacred Heart Mission on the Register without interference from the Roman Catholic Church.

5. See Page 9, of Respondent's Comments.
6. See Page I, of Respondent's Comments.

-3-

To allow the Roman Catholic Church to interfere with the
placement of Sacred Heart Mission Church on the National Register is
violative of the First Amendment to the United States Constitution:

> Congress shall make no law respecting an
> establishment of religion, or prohibiting
> the free exercise thereof; or abridging the
> freedom of speech, or of the press; or the
> right of the people peaceably to assemble,
> and to petition the Government for a redress
> of grievances.

III.

FACT CLARIFICATION

The Respondent misstates the facts [7] concerning the timing of landmark status:

> The constitutional problems become acute
> when the effort to achieve landmark designa-
> tion occurs in the course of an active
> controversy over whether or not a church
> should continue to function.

The effort to achieve landmark status was initiated by John R. Downs, a citizen of Illinois, on July 28, 1978, when application was made to the Chicago Historical and Architectural Landmark Commission. This was long before the surprise closing of Sacred Heart Mission Church, which occured approximately six (6) months later.

The legal "controversy" between Petitioner and Respondent was laid to rest when the United States Supreme Court denied, without comment, Petitioner's Petition for Certiorari. [8]

The Acting City Planner of the City of Chicago, on May 5, 1980, served a letter on the Chicago Landmark Commission recommending inter alia that Sacred Heart not be considered for nomination since Sacred Heart was removed from the National Register. [9]

Thus, the temporary removal of Sacred Heart Mission Church from the National Register has already had potentially dire consequences.

The Department of the Interior is not being asked by Petitioner to overturn Respondent's decision to close Sacred Heart Mission Church. This is a misstatement of fact.

7. See Page 9 of Respondent's Comments.
8. See Petitioner's Petition to the United States Supreme Court for Certiorari.
9. See Letter from Martin Murphy, Acting City Planner of City of Chicago.

-5-

Petitioner is asking that the Department of the Interior return Sacred Heart Mission Church to the National Register where it belongs. No lightning will come from the sky; the Bishop's administration will not be infiltrated by government agents.

In short, no harm will befall anyone. The thunderings of fear Respondent conjures by threatening that the Department of the Interior..."will be plunging deeply into a religious controversy,"[10] is without foundation.

Respondent, through its intimidation of elected government officials, is now seeking to interfere with the Government, this is expressly prohibited by the First Amendment. The religious liberty which the Constitution protects does not exclude legislation of general scope not directed against doctrinal loyalties of particular sects.

Respondent states, on Page 12:

> "The Government is excluded entirely from religious matters."

The reverse is also true; Religion should not force its might, (holy though it may be), on Government.

10. See Page 11 of Respondent's Comments.

IV.

ARCHITECTURAL AND HISTORIC DISTINCTION

The Department of the Interior has already decided upon the recommendation of the Illinois Department of Conservation, that Sacred Heart Mission Church should be honored by placement on the National Register.

Respondent concedes on Page 13, that there is no debate concerning the landmark designation:

> "In brief, this nomination does not
> present a controversy over architectural
> or historical distinction."

Petitioner entirely agrees.

Respondent's attempt to interject "religious controversy" is a blatant attempt to have the Roman Catholic Church direct the policies of the Department of the Interior.

In Abington School District v. Schempp, 374 U.S. 203, 259, 83 S. Ct. 1560, 1591, 10 L. Ed. 2d 844 (1963), Justice Brennan succinctly stated that:

> "government and religion have discrete interests
> which are mutually best served when each avoids
> too close a proximity to the other." See also
> Rhode Island Federation of Teachers v. Norberg,
> 479 F. Supp. 1364 (1979).

V.

CONCLUSION

———

Petitioner incorporates by reference all documents submitted to the Department of the Interior by the Illinois Department of Conservation, Beverly Planning Association and all other documents previously submitted on behalf of the designation of Sacred Heart Mission Church for listing on the National Register of Historic Places.

"Honor" is a word seldom used in our society today. Yet, "honor" is what the National Register is all about. To honor buildings that are part of the history of America is to honor the essence of America.

Sacred Heart Mission Church is such a building. Because of its history in the development of America and significance in the State of Illinois and the City of Chicago it deserves the honor of designation in the National Register.

Sacred Heart Mission Church is a historic place. Honor it once more and for always, please.

Respectfully Submitted,

O'DONNELL & MURPHY

BY: _____
    Sheila Murphy

Attorneys for Petitioner
55 East Monroe-Suite 4005
Chicago, Illinois   60603
(312) 263-5747

Two Letters Out of Many Which Plea for the Preservation of Sacred Heart Shrine. The First is from the Association of Franco-Americans and the Second is from Three Supporters of Sacred Heart Church Directed to Pope John Paul II

Assemblée des Franco-Américains/Association of Franco-Americans
University of Rhode Island
Kingston, R.I. 02881

President
Professor Armand B. Chartier
Department of Languages
University of Rhode Island
Kingston, R.I. 02881
  (401) 792-5911
  (401) 789-4165 (Res.)

First Vice-President
Mr. Homer Dyess
Louisiana State Dept. of Education
P.O. Box 44064
Baton Rouge, Louisiana 70804
  (504) 342-3454

Northeast Regional Vice-President
Mr. Stéphane Duplessis
F.A.R.O.G. – Fernald Hall
University of Maine
Orono, Maine 04469
  (207) 581-7082

Southern Regional Vice-President
Mr. René Calais
National Bilingual Resource Center
P.O. Box 43410
University of Southwestern Louisiana
Lafayette, Louisiana 70504
  (318) 264-6991

North Central Regional Vice-President
Mme Marie-Reine Mikesell
1155 East 56th St.
Chicago, Illinois 60637
  (312) 643-7865

Secretary
Mr. David Veilleux
St. John Valley Bilingual Program
P.O. Box 210
Madawaska, Maine 04576
  (207) 728-4849

Treasurer
Mr. Richard J. Guidry
141 Avon Court
Breaux Bridge, Louisiana 70517
  (318) 332-4733

At-Large Board Members
Soeur Cécile Brassard
Rural Education Center
Trinity College
Burlington, Vermont 05401
  (802) 658-6342

Mr. Robert Sullivan
North-American Cattle Company
911 Champs-Elysées
New Orleans, Louisiana 70117
  (504) 945-2947

Publicity Coordinator
Ms. Jeannine T. Lévesque
Nashua Telegraph
60 Main St.
Nashua, New Hampshire 03060
  (603) 882-2741
  (603) 889-0226 (Res.)

Legal Counsel
Walter J. Landry, Esq.
425 West Vermilion St.
Lafayette, Louisiana 70501
  (318) 237-5911

September 5, 1980

The Honorable Jane M. Byrne
Mayor of the City of Chicago
City Hall
121 N. LaSalle Street
Chicago, Illinois 60602

Your Honor:

In the city of Chicago there is a French mission church--the last one built in the United States--which is threatened with demolition. Different in essence from parish churches, French mission churches served as outposts of Civilization on the 'western' frontier. The French Mission Church of Sacred Heart located in the former village of Morgan Park is associated with 300 years of French presence in the region of the Great Lakes. It is remarkable that it could have survived in the second metropolis of the nation.

As National President of the Association of Franco-Americans, I would be profoundly grateful for your help in preserving this testimony to our past.

Yours sincerely,

Armand B. Chartier, Ph.D.
President, AFA

ABC:KJ

January 23, 1979

His Holiness Pope John Paul II
Apostolic Munciature Delegation
Aveneda Maximo Gomez #27
Apt. Postal 312
Cable # Nuntius
Santo Domingo,
Dominican Republic

Your Holiness, we beg for your ultimate intercession to save the
Sacred Heart Church, 11652 S. Church Street, Chicago, Illinois 60643

The spirit of this outstanding mission Church has endured and flourished
since 1902 largely through the dedicated efforts of the Pastors who have
been assigned. Father Kenneth Borchardt having been the most recent
great inspirator.

Suddenly, this past week-end, John Cardinal Cody announced that the Church
would be immediately shut down and demolished, even though it is self-sustaining
with upwards of a 1000 good Catholics attending its weekly masses.

Your Holiness was recently quoted in the U.S. press as follows, "Going
back to your homes, your schools, and your associations, tell everyone
that the Pope counts greatly on young people. Tell them that young people
are the comfort and strength of the Pope, who wants to see them all."

We assure you, Your Holiness, that Sacred Heart Church reflects a sea of young
high school student faces every week. They shine out among the faces of those
in attendance who were in school a few years back. But who's counting?

We pray that you will find the time, somehow, within your busy schedule,
to counsel John Cardinal Cody and encourage him to give this most
important decision another measure of consideration.

                            The most humble supporters of the
                            Sacred Heart Church
                            % Andrew Galich
                               300 W. Washington
                               Chicago, Illinois, 60606

                               Arthur Quinn
                               3044 W. 119th Street
                               Merrionette Park, Illinois, 60658

                               John R. Downs
                               11555 S. Maplewood Avenue
                               Chicago, Illinois 60655

N/B- above message dictated to New Jersey Western Union office at 2:06 pm Chicago time,
1/24/79 Maggie Weiss, took dictation(excellent read back, including all punctuation)
     Copy of message as sent will be sent to us for record and confirmation of delivery.
                                            JRD

An August 24, 1979 Copy of Monsignor Francis A. Brackin's
Response to the National Register of Historic Places Stating
the Position of the Archdiocese Regarding the Closing of Sacred Heart

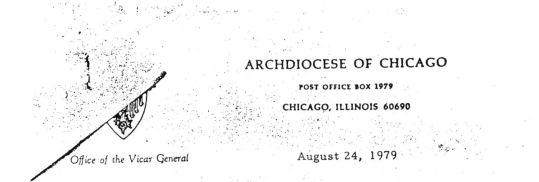

ARCHDIOCESE OF CHICAGO

POST OFFICE BOX 1979

CHICAGO, ILLINOIS 60690

Office of the Vicar General   August 24, 1979

Mr. Charles Herrington
Acting Keeper of the National
  Register of Historic Places
  Heritage Conservation
Department of the Interior
Pension Building
440 "G" Street, N. W.
Washington, D. C. 20243

Dear Mr. Herrington:

According to the rules and regulations of your jurisduction,
I am formally objecting to the listing of the Shrine of the Sacred Heart
(Chicago, Ill.) on the National Register of Historic Places.

The owner of record, the Archdiocese of Chicago, does not
believe that this edifice meets the high standards of the National Register,
and that it was recommended to you by the Illinois Historic Preservation
Officer because of intense lobbying and pressure.

The nomination form is incorrect in several respects. The
status of the building is not that it is "occupied", it is unoccupied. The
nomination form says that it is "accessible", in fact it is inaccessible. The
church was closed January 21, 1979. Its present use is not "religious". It
is not being used at all. Its condition is not "good". It has substantial problems which would require substantial funds to correct. As noted on the
form, the building has been "altered".

This building is not an important structure. You will note
that on areas of significance only "religion" and "other", namely "history"
were checked. It was not recommended for either "art" or "architecture".
It is not unique. (There is another French Church which has also been
nominated to the National Register, namely Notre Dame of Chicago). The
original structure as the nomination states was entirely of wood. It was
later veneered with brick. There is no specific architectural style as the
nomination form admits. Reference is made to 14 stained glass windows.
They are not the work of Lewis Comfort Tiffany, nor his studios. It is
clear that the edifice is not worthy of nomination.

Mr. Charles Herrington
August 24, 1979
Page 2

As to its history, being a building of this century, there is very little. Certainly, there is none that would distinguish it from any other church, frankly, of any other denomination. The fact that Charles Walgreen III, still a young man, played the organ of that church, or that a former Chicago fire commissioner who passed on recently also attended services there does not seem to us to be sufficient for entry of this building on the National Register.

Under separate cover, we are sending photographs of the interior and exterior that substantiate our position. We respectfully urge that you decline to list this building on the National Register of Historic Places and so notify Mr. David Kenny, Illinois Historic Preservation Officer. We, of course, stand ready to answer any further inquiries that you may have, but it is our opinion that this building clearly does not deserve your designation.

Sincerely yours,

Rev. Msgr. Francis A. Brackin
Vicar General

cc: Mr. William Brabham
Registered Mail

A Letter from Illinois Governor James Thompson Regarding
the Battle to Save Sacred Heart. This is One of the Many
Received By the Committee That Disheartened Those Keeping a Vigil

STATE OF ILLINOIS
OFFICE OF THE GOVERNOR
SPRINGFIELD 62706

JAMES R. THOMPSON
GOVERNOR

February 13, 1979

Mrs. Douglas J. Tatro
11702 S. Oakley Avenue
Chicago, Il   60643

Dear Mrs. Tatro:

Your letter to the Governor concerning the Sacred Heart
of Shrine Church located at 11652 So. Church Street,
Chicago was referred to my office for review and any
possible action.

I am sorry to inform you that there is nothing that
the Governor's Office could do in this instance, it is
owned by the church and that is their prerogative to
do with it as they see fit.

If my office can ever be of further service, do not
hesitate to call on us.

Sincerely,

Richard W. Mowery, Director
Governor's Information Agency

RWM/dm

Two Letters from Marie-Reine Mikesell, A Chicago Journalist and of
French Descent Concerning Her Efforts to Preserve French History

February 10, 1980

A.E.P. Wall, editor
The Chicago Catholic
155 E. Superior Street
Chicago, Illinois 60611

Dear Sir:

Please permit me to answer your editorial of February 8, 1980.
Contrary to what is said in this article, the nomination of the French
mission to the National Register is not the result of political pressure
but rather is based on solid historical reasoning.

The first Europeans in this part of the country were the French.
They came in the Midwest as early as 1634. It was the French missionaries
who planted christianity in the Great Lakes area and the whole Mississippi
Valley. On the site of Chicago the French presence goes back to 1673 with
the explorer Louis Jolliet and the missionary Father Jacques Marquette.
They were on their way back from the discovery of the Mississippi River.
Many other explorers and missionaries followed in their footsteps, putting
the site of Chicago at the crossroads of the history of French explorations
in the West.

On the site of Chicago a series of three French mission churches were
built. The first one, called "L'Ange Gardien" (Guardian Angel), goes back
to 1696. Of the three, only the last one is still standing. This mission
church is Sacred Heart. And it is today and for the future generations
the only tangible reminder of the heroic missionary past. Since French
missionaries accompanied French explorers in their discovery of the American
West, they must be considered not only as priests but also as key actors
in the drama of the history of America.

Unfortunately few people know the history of the French missionaries,
their work, their sufferings and their pains. They did not all die of
exhaustion at thirty years of age, as was the case of Father Jacques
Marquette. About twelve of them died, at various times, after a dreadful
agony, carved up and burned alive according to the Indian custom of those
times.

For all they did, for all they were, the Church has an obligation to
keep their memory alive. In Chicago --the historic door to the West--
the humble church of Sacred Heart is the keeper of the flame.

Sincerely,

Marie-Reine Mikesell

Marie-Reine Mikesell
1155 East 56th Street
Chicago, Illinois 60637

cc: Jack Houston, religion editor
    Chicago Tribune

April 4, 1980

Mr. Christian Delaporte, Director
US Department of the Interior,
Heritage Conservation and Recreation Service,
Washington D.C. 20243

Re: <u>Sacred Heart Shrine in Chicago</u>

Dear Mr. Delaporte,

    I am a journalist and I write articles for various newspapers on the history of the United States and more specifically on the history of the Midwest. I realized sometime ago that the catholic hierarchy in our city had no knowledge of the French background of this region, which was French for two centuries before the arrival of the "Bostonians" as all Americans were then called by the French. Ever since I had been looking for an opportunity to put some light on this subject.

    I thought I had found it when I answered an editorial in the <u>Chicago Catholic</u> (February 8, 1980) condemning "the interference of Illinois politicians in the affairs of the Church". Enclosed is my letter and its published version. As you will see, it decries lack of fairness and the depriving of the readers of that newspaper of the right to a judgment on a controversy that has been in the news continously during the last fourteen months. I have myself gathered 169 press clippings, but there are many more as the chairman of Save Our Historic Shrine (SOHS) has just sent a dossier of 402 press items to a national TV network, at its request, to be used as background in the making of a documentary. Also, the "Maison Française" of Chicago, which sponsors tours of historic French sites in this city, has put the mission on its itinerary.

    In Canada the surviving churches of the type of the Chicago French Mission have been preserved as a testimony to the history of that country and are being serviced not by parish priests but by religious orders.

    John Cardinal Cody, head of the diocese of Chicago, is over 72 years of age. He will have to step down the year of his 75th birthday according to the new regulations of Pope Paul VI. In view of the difficulties experienced by the diocese during the last ten years, I do not doubt that the Apostolic Delegate in Washington, D.C. will then recommand the appointment of a more sensitive prelate.

                          Sincerely,

                          Marie-Reine Mikesell

                          Marie-Reine Mikesell
                          1155 East 56th Street
                          Chicago, Illinois 60637

Encl. 3

cc: Carol D. Shull
    acting keeper of the National Register

Part IV

The Changing Face of Chicago's Parishes,
1911-1940

"New groups arrive, each one with a different history,
to settle here and become part of something new...E Pluribus Unum."

-Pope John Paul II

St. Bonaventure
1641 W. Diversey, Chicago, Illinois

St. Bonaventure, officially established October 11, 1911, was another example of an immigrant church originally established in the Lake View area on the north side of Chicago to relieve the overcrowding in nearby parishes, particularly St. Alphonsus. The first pastor, Rev. Martin J. McGuire, quickly went about contracting Joseph Mollitor, the architect, and a skilled group of artisans led by Chief Mason Van Etten and Head Carpenter L. Baleb, to begin construction on the Romanesque church. By August 18, 1912 Bishop Rhode was able to lay the church cornerstone and by June 8, 1913 Archbishop Quigley dedicated the new church. The same year the Sisters of St. Joseph of LaGrange, Illinois opened the parish school which grew to such an extent that by 1951 additional wooden classrooms needed to be added. A new school was built in 1953 and dedicated on April 11, 1954, which was necessitated by the rapid growth of parish families. Even during the worst years of the depression, this parish of hard working immigrant laborers flourished and their children were educated so that they might enjoy jobs which could outlast the depths of depression.

By 1966 a significant number of Latino residents joined the German and Italian families already in the parish. African-Americans became the fourth large immigrant group by the early 1920s, creating a multiethnic parish that remained a close knit, giving Catholic fraternity. Their generosity was demonstrated in 1972 when they gave sufficiently to renovate and redecorate the the deteriorating church interior. Two years later the parish debt had also been retired. The school today is operated by lay faculty as the Sisters of St. Joseph withdrew in 1975.

St. Bonaventure's Romanesque architecture is highlighted by a 125 x 65 foot building whose front is unusually broad with twin bell towers rising from the fourth level but which are not distinct entities in and of themselves. Seven square windows with a modified Greek key design ornament the first two floors and contain within each beautiful stained glass scenes. The third level contains an additional five windows, all of which are double side by side windows surrounded by brick molding. The twin bell towers each contain twelve arched windows with a matching semicircular brick topping to highlight the grace and beauty of the spires. The beautifully carved wooden entrance doors are crowned with stained glass windows depicting religious motifs and reflecting a rainbow of light down the center aisle. The simple beauty of the workmanship reflects the depth of faith held by those immigrants who brought St. Bonaventure's to life.

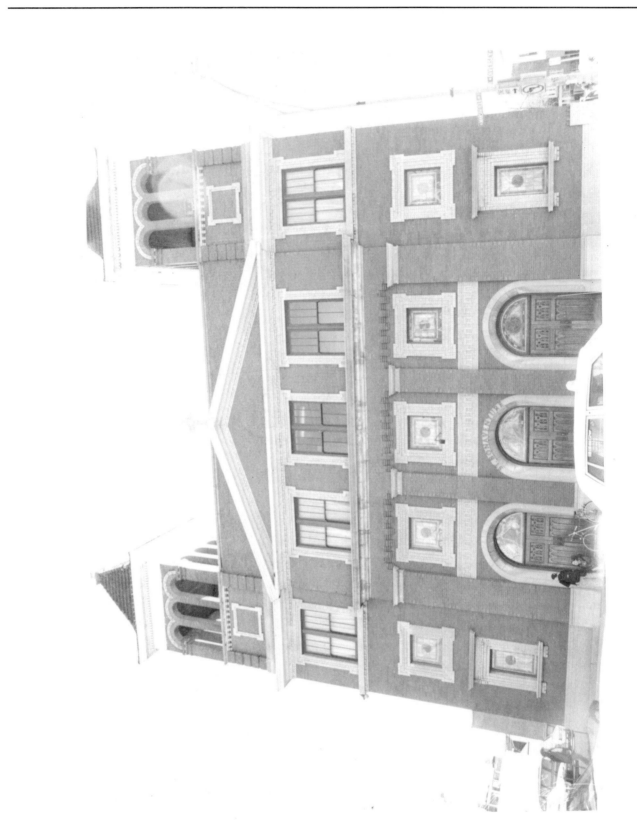

The broad Romanesque style of architecture highlights the front facade of St. Bonaventure.

The window borders of St. Bonaventure show the intricate brick work
which shadowcases the stained glass windows.

The entranceway to St. Bonaventure shows the blending of intricately carved wood doors, the stained glass semicircular windows, and the strength of the stonecutters art.

St. Philip Neri
2131 E. 72nd Street, Chicago, Ill.

It was 1912 and just west of the Lake Michigan breezes, in a middle class neighborhood of brick working men's homes, a new parish was needed. Irish immigrants were moving into the area south of Jackson Park and sought out a parish church and school for their children's education and religious training. The bases for both were firmly laid with the dedication of the newly completed church on April 26, 1914. Within five years, 400 families were being served by the church and the new school, staffed by the Dominican Sisters of Adrian, Michigan, was furiously enrolling new children. Both the church and school blossomed from the start. During the week Irish children tramped with bagged lunches to the 16 room school to pour over the catechism, English grammar, history and mathematics. The liberal arts were blended with scripture to produce the well-rounded Catholic scholar. On Sundays, the all male Chaneel Choir sang the liturgy with a fervor not lost on the faithful who filled its pews. Many a passerby could be lifted away by the Gregorian chants and the hymns of the Motu Proprio. At the altar Father William J. Kinsella, who had celebrated the first Mass at St. Philip Neri, was intoning the final Pater Noster to a bowed and reverent congregation who lived its faith and loved its neighborhood church. This reverence was reflected in the simple grace and beauty of the brick church—the cornerstone of the immigrant neighborhood.

The imposing edifice of St. Philip Neri. Note the spire, ornate in design, rising from the center with a majesty pointing the faithful to heaven.

The magnificent carvings over the front entranceway of St. Philip Neri highlight various coat of arms, fleur-de-lis, and flower patterns. The workmanship was a lasting tribute to the immigrant artisans.

Dr. Marie Rudisch of Austria, one of the members of the St. Philip Neri church council, has taken pride in her church since first immigrating to America.

St. Gertrude
1420 W. Granville, Chicago, Illinois

As the North Edgewater area of Chicago began to receive a large influx of new Irish and German immigrant families, the need for a parish to relieve the overcrowding of St. Ignatius and St. Ita became readily apparent to Archbishop Quigley. Thus, on January 3, 1912 Father Peter F. Shrewbridge was named the first pastor of St. Gertrude's and began the planning of the Gothic marvel that was to dominate the neighborhood, then consisting of only scattered housing, no sidewalks and overgrown prairie lots. While the plans for the permanent church took shape, the needs of the parish families were by a portable wood and steel frame church brought on site. It was here the first Palm Sunday services in the parish were held on March 31, 1912.

The parish school was temporarily housed in a private home on Granville Avenue operated by the Sisters of Charity of the Blessed Virgin Mary from Dubuque, Iowa. Enrollment immediately accelerated and the new pastor, Father Bernard Heeney had to put the permanent church on hold and begin plans for a new three story brick combination church and school to house parish religious services and schoolchildren. This new combination facility, church on the first floor, school on the second and third, and chapel in the basement was to serve the parish well for the next decade.

Again however a population surge after World War I saw school enrollment soar to 480 children and parish families increase church capacity to the breaking point. Fr. Heeney swung into high gear and the church family began an almost nonstop series of fundraisers—socials, teas, card parties, bake sales and bazaars to raise money for the construction of a permanent church, a rectory, and a convent. The rectory and convent, designed by noted architect James Burns, were completed in 1929, just prior to the Great Depression. But the generosity of the church members, and their contributions of time and labor, were only slowed by the hard economic times not stopped. James Burns continued with his building of the massive Gothic church where stained glass windows crafted by Franz Mayer of Munich, Germany ringed the exterior, an $18,000 Kilgen organ filtered beautiful Gregorian chants through the aisles, and five altars of Carrara marble ornamented, "with gold mosaics and Pavonazzo trimmings," called the faithful forward for the Eucharist.

The exterior was a matching architectural tribute to the faith of its early founders. The Gothic bell tower was a reminder of a medieval castle tower with eight long, narrow windows divided by ornamentation of the most meticulous design and crowned with four miniature towers and statues on each side. The doors of solid wood were topped with stained glass, ornamental rosettes, and heavy iron accoutrements. A connecting open passageway (now the entrance to the Ministry Center), recalled for the passerby the hallways of Europe's great cathedrals and the visitor could almost see hooded monks scampering to vespers through the drafty corridors. The church was strong, massive, ornate and symbolic of the enduring faith of its builders.

Today St. Gertrude's is a multiethnic parish which has retained some of its Irish and German founders and has added African-American, Polish, Hispanic, Chinese, Filipino, Hungarian, Italian, Japanese, Lithuanian and Vietnamese Catholics to its diverse body. Activities of the parish have attempted to include all of these groups and the school board, parish council, and organizations are reflective of this great diversity.

St. Gertrude's is an awe inspiring example of Gothic architecture
designed by noted architect James Burns.

The connecting walkway of St. Gertrude's reminds the visitor of the European cathedrals and processions of solemn monks going to matins.

The rectory door of St. Gertrude's reflects the solid wood, stained glass, and strong lines of the Gothic style.

St. Sabina's
1210 W. 78th Place, Chicago, Ill.

In the second decade of the Twentieth Century, the Catholic Archdiocese of Chicago was in the midst of an unprecedented wave of expansion necessitated by the seemingly endless stream of new immigrants to Chicago. One of the areas experiencing a great influx of new Catholics was Auburn Highlands, a compact blue collar residential area bounded by 75th and 83rd Streets and by Aberdeen and Ashland Avenues. It was here that the first Pastor, Rev. T.F. Egan, began his task in earnest, celebrating the first mass in July of 1916 in a small store front shop near 79th and Ashland Ave. By the following month, attendance was so great that the little church-to-be moved to an abandoned store at 7743 Racine Avenue, where church attendees soon outstripped the capacity of this location, forcing four separate masses to be held on Sunday. As the plans for the permanent site proceeded, so too did the quest for a school so that the children could obtain an education imbued with Catholicism.

On December 8, 1916 ground was broken for the new church and immediately the architectural firm of Steinbuck & Davis began the slow wintry construction. Throughout the same severe winter of 1916-1917, workmen labored to get the church ready for the laying of the cornerstone on May 13, 1917 by Rev. A. J. McGavick, D.D. From this point on the parish experienced the phenomenal growth associated with a bulging immigrant influx. Children filled the classrooms at the new school and the Dominican Sisters of Sinsinawa threw themselves into staffing the ever-expanding classes of eager learners. Today, the church serves the same neighborhood, still a working class southside enclave, but populated overwhelmingly by African Americans. Its architectural simplicity stressing functional strength of design stands today as a mute testimony to its immigrant beginnings.

St. Sabina's Church is a splendid example of simplicity of design highlighting strength of character so reminiscent of immigrants to Chicago.

The magnificent wooden doors of St. Sabina's are highlighted by small panes of glass which reflect the nearby trees and scenes in a peaceful repose.

The statue of Christ overlooks the massive wooden doors at the entrance to St. Sabina's. Note the intricate carved lattice work and the crowning cupola over the statue where detail was savored.

St. Claret de Montefalco
5443 S. Washtenaw Ave., Chicago, Illinois

It was 1909 and the Augustinian priests of South Chicago's Gage Park neighborhood realized that immigration was proceeding unabated. The need for a new church and school to relieve the pressure from neighboring parishes like St. Gall was mounting. Polish immigrants were arriving for jobs in the Union Stock Yards and nearby manufacturing plants. Thus the Archdiocese gave Father James F. Green permission to found St. Clare's as a mission with permanent status to follow shortly thereafter. On August 8, 1909 the cornerstone was laid and the church dedicated on January 30, 1910. By September of that same year, the parish children were attending school under the tutelage of Adrian Dominican nuns.

By 1923 the combination mission church and school again proved too small and the pastor, Rev. J.J. Barthouski, received permission to build a new church structure. Within five years, the parish had grown to 2,000 worshippers and saw 425 children attending the school (which had to again be expanded in 1929). But this was not to be the last period of explosive parish growth. Following World War II, the baby boomers added new faithful to the parish rolls necessitating the construction of the present church, which was begun in November of 1953. It was dedicated two years later on November 6, 1955 by Cardinal Stritch. This new church came none too soon as new parishioners, now principally German, Irish, Italian, Lithuanian and Hispanic continued to arrive to claim the neighborhood's neat little homes and two flats. The parish today remains ethically diverse and continues to welcome new arrivals as it did in 1979 when the parish hung out a huge 18 foot sign proclaiming, "Welcome Home."

The present St. Clare de Montefalco is of modern Gothic design with a cut stone front facade highlighted by a four door double entrance contained within a massive arched plate glass and pillared entranceway. Four stone columns divide the entrance and have a unique companion stone design of eight smaller pillars atop the carved doors. Two small windows to the left and right of the main entrance balance each other in wonderful symmetry. Side panels consist of intricately carved grape vines in relief, giving a sense of ornateness tempered by gracefulness. All of the major window areas are highlighted by stained glass motifs denoting scenes of religious significance and mystery. While this parish has gone through three churches and as many schools and additions, it remains a beacon for ethnic diversity on Chicago's south side.

St. Clare de Montefalco exhibits several of these intricately carved side panels depicting grape vines inset into stone.

Mrs. Frech's class at St. Clare de Montefalco represents the wonderful mix of cultures that have added strength to the parish over the years.

St. Clare de Montefalco is an example of modern Gothic design set in a neighborhood of ethnic diversity and representing the hard work and toil of numerous ethnic immigrants.

St. Barnabas
10134 S. Longwood Ave., Chicago, Illinois

The Beverly Hills area of Chicago, a neighborhood characterized by stately turn-of-the-century homes built by many whose names were prominent in the social and business history of Chicago, was an area dominated by Protestant churches in the 1920s. Almost all of these churches had large, "well-heeled" congregations. While Catholic families were scarce in this area, they were moving in in increasing numbers, becoming a force in the settling of the area. Principally Irish, they welcomed their first pastor, the Rev. Timothy J. Hurley, also Irish-American, in the spring of 1924. After area residents prevented Father Hurley's first choice of sites for a church from becoming a reality by condemning the land for a park, he was ultimately successful in acquiring a home and vacant land within two blocks of his original choice. But the construction he planned for his new Irish parish was not to be easy.

In July 1924, the Ku Klux Klan conducted a ritualistic cross burning in front of the combination church and school under construction. The buildings themselves suffered no damage but the sentiments of the neighborhood were evident and slow to change. Father Hurley however was not to be deterred. The cornerstone for the new church was laid on October 15, 1924 and on December 25, 1924 the first mass was celebrated. As had virtually every immigrant parish in Chicago, St. Barnabas founded a school which opened in January 1925. Staffed by the Dominican Sisters of Sinsinawa, Wisconsin, they set about their work of providing a Catholic education to an increasing number of new parish children.

Through the next several decades, St. Barnabas continued to grow, even though the parish boundaries were reduced in size. A new convent was built in 1947, a Victorian Beverly home was acquired for a rectory the same year and a new 24 room school was built in 1958. Designed by Joseph McCarthy and Associates, it could hold 1,050 students, a stunning growth in the few decades since the Klan tried to prevent the parish from ever beginning. These structures served the parish well. But in 1966, Father Norbert O'Connell, the new pastor, announced their beloved church was being torn down as structurally dangerous. The present church, designed by McCarthy-Hundriesen and Associates, and completed in 1969, is of modern design with stone columns resembling pillars across the front, wooden entrance doors with long elongated windows, and an abundance of carvings and statues of a sleek, modern style. Simplicity is the rule, but the old is not forgotten. Rather, it has been "updated" to fit contemporary styles and tastes. The parish today is still predominately Irish but now also numbers among its parishioners African-Americans, Germans and small numbers of other nationalities. Together, they have kept the parish and school thriving and the parish organizations active and vital. To Fr. Hurley's credit the unwelcome sign he rejected in 1924 now reads "Welcome" at the front door to all who enter to worship.

The modern architectural design of St. Barnabas is modeled after the more traditional but with the sleek lines and open spaces of the new.

St. Barnabas displays this ultra modern example of religious art as one of many that adorn this south side Irish parish.

A wonderful carved rendition of St. Barnabas graces the brick wall in a protective
pose of reflection and wisdom.

Market day at St. Barnabas. These sales of bulk food act as an example of modern fundraising so vital to area parishes.

St. Ethelreda Church
8754 S. Paulina Ave., Chicago, Illinois

St. Ethelreda's was a young Irish parish in the days of Al Capone and Bugs Moran. As new immigrants moved south from the area of the Union Stock Yards and west of St. Kilian's parish to take jobs at the steel mills and factories of the growing south side of Chicago, the Archdiocese saw the need for a new parish to cater to their religious needs. Finally, as the number of Irish families increased to the point where a parish could be sustained, Cardinal George Mundelein gave permission to Father John L. O'Donnell to organize the new parish. He immediately rented a workman's bungalow at 8824 S. Marshfield, held mass in the basement, and hired the architect Joe W. McCarthy to design the new church and an accompanying school. On March 19, 1927 the ground was broken for the combination church and school and construction proceeded so quickly that the church was ready to be dedicated by November 6 of the same year. The Sisters of Mercy opened the parish school in September of 1927 and within three years two hundred students were in attendance. By 1930, that number had grown to 328 children from 1,500 parish families.

Through the next two decades and World War II, membership in the Irish parish continued to increase. The first St. Ethelreda's church and school would no longer hold the faithful and educate their children. Thus, on March 23, 1952 the pastor, Fr. William R. Leyhane broke ground for the second, and current, St. Ethelreda's. The cornerstone was laid on September 21, 1952 and Cardinal Stritch dedicated the new church on May 17, 1953. This new church and school combination served the parish well for another two decades, even seeing the enrollment at the parish school climb to 750 children. But then in the early 1970s the early Irish settlers began moving further south and west to the fringes of Chicago and to the adjacent suburbs. African-American residents moved into the parish and now comprise the total composition of the church. But St. Ethelreda's still serves its new community well, with activities, community concern and a devotion to the area's families. The new St. Ethelreda's is of modern design with a triple entranceway square in design with a triple statue arrangement atop the front doors. The light brown brick and large square front design lends a symmetrical oneness to the two side extensions. A large cross runs upward from the central doorway and culminates in an ornate stained glass window. Above is a cross and carved marble statue of St. Ethelreda beckoning all to come in and enjoy the PAX (peace) so boldly inscribed on the rectory facade.

St. Ethelreda's is an old Irish parish that has successfully adopted its new African-American congregation and retained its vibrancy.

The rectory of St. Ethelreda's shows the modern simplicity of light brick. The stairway however shows the modern decay that is threatening the building.

The ornately carved PAX symbol on the rectory facade of St. Ethelreda's beckons all to come in peace to the house of the Lord.

St. Cajetan Church
112th and Artesian Avenue, Chicago, Illinois

From the first mass held in Clissold Public School on July 3, 1927, the small frame church that followed, and finally the new modern brick building, the parishioners of St. Cajetan's have been well served. At its inception St. Cajetan's served the Morgan Park area of Chicago, a neighborhood on the extreme southwest corner of the city. In fact, the immigrants to this area did not even become part of Chicago until 1914. Its prairies, middle class bungalows, apartment buildings and hard working shopkeepers and tradesmen were principally Irish and German.

In 1935, the small parish still only contained 150 families but the prediction was that this corner of Chicago would soon see a serge of brick homes, small businesses and families with children eager for a Catholic education. Thus, on March 19, 1936 ground was broken for a parish school. Designed by architect Gerald A. Barry and staffed by the Dominican Sisters of Sinsinawa, Wisconsin, the school soon proved its worth. Children began enrolling in large numbers as the parish population increased to a size requiring the frame church to triple in size.

But this was not to be the last expansion. In 1947 the rectory was enlarged, in 1948 a school addition and combination church was dedicated, a new convent was completed in 1951, a new primary school was built in 1955, and on June 4, 1961 ground was broken for the present church, a modern brick and stone design by the firm of Barry and Kay. By this time, 1800 families were served by the parish and school enrollment soared to 1020. But this unprecedented growth was still to continue. By 1969 the parish began a six year crusade for donations that saw a new rectory built, the addition of a gymnasium and a social center, and the remodeling of the church sanctuary in a Gothic style, one of the few churches of Chicago whose modern exterior contained within a Gothic splendor reminiscent of the European roots of many of its parishioners. The faithful of the parish gave to all of these projects willingly, pledging their paychecks to see all of these new projects through. And yet, more families came. By 1977 the parish topped 2,000 families but school enrollment declined to 655 children, due mostly to the general social trend of having smaller families. It was also at this time that, as had occurred in virtually all of Chicago's immigrant parishes, the exclusivity of ethnic makeup changed. To join the Irish and German founders of the church came the Polish, Lithuanian, Filipino, Hispanic and African-American faithful. The new ethnic diversity however has been welcomed and the parish today has a stable population and a dedicated congregation. The church and school of simple modern architecture still contain the stained glass, carvings, niches, crosses and ornamentation that convey a sense of Gothic glory to those who enter the church through its three front doors or the school by climbing the two sets of six steps each and passing beneath the archway formed by two overhanging trees. The sense of peace and dignity is present in both buildings and in the people who built this southwest side immigrant parish.

St. Cajetan church displays modern architecture but retains a sanctuary of Gothic design
so beloved by the early Irish and German founders of the parish.

The exterior Gothic statue holder of St. Cajetan's school is highlighted by the trees which arch over the entranceway in a peaceful greeting to all who enter.

Holy Name of Mary
112th and Loomis, Chicago, Illinois

As the 1940s dawned on the Archdiocese of Chicago, changes in the ethnic mix of the city created a new immigrant group of Catholics in many areas of the city, African-Americans. Holy Name of Mary was created specifically for this new immigrant group at 112th and Loomis Street and, when formed, served only twenty-five black families. As black Catholics were generally still unwelcome in 1940 in neighboring parishes, Cardinal Stritch made the decision to build a new parish rather than force integration. In September 1940, Father John F. Ryan was named as the first pastor and plans were drawn up for a temporary combination church and school building. The school would be staffed by the Oblate Sisters of Providence, a black order of nuns from Baltimore, Maryland. This would truly be a parish not previously tried by the Archdiocese, i.e. one planned, designed, and intended for the use of black Catholics. With financial assistance from the Archdiocese, the church was completed and dedicated by Cardinal Stritch on November 8, 1942.

Within a decade, Holy Name of Mary, never a wealthy parish, nevertheless was able to construct a new convent dedicated by Cardinal Stritch on April 15, 1951. This enabled the parish priests to reclaim their rectory as living quarters. A brick church hall, built by the men of the parish, was added in 1954. Throughout the period 1954-1964 the new pastor, Father James W. Keating, worked to provide services to the parishioners, assist outlying missions and discharge the parish debt. The school, numbering 458 children by 1965, continued to provide an excellent education to the youngsters of the parish.

By 1970 Holy Name of Mary was finally prepared, financially and by strength of the congregation size, to break ground for a separate church. This event was hailed by the pastor, Rev. Anthony J. Vader, who has chosen to spend his retirement years at Holy Name of Mary, as a momentous event for the parish as it was to be the first black parish with its own church in the Archdiocese of Chicago. Sensing the important nature of the event, Fr. Vader and the Archdiocese attempted to design the church with the parishioners in mind. A black construction company, Bush Construction Co., and a black architect, Raymond Broady, were retained for the project. They were joined by black Professor Carl W. Merschel, who served as overall design-artist and was charged with creating the mosaics utilized in the church vestibule and on the baptismal font and black artist Frank Hayden who designed the fiberglass Madonna and the panels of beatitudes. A Nigerian artist, Francis Osague, designed an African Madonna reminiscent of the parishioners' roots and Andre Vitez produced the beautiful Stations of the Cross. Additional stained glass work portraying African-American art decorate the exterior walls and alcoves. Carvings of Mary and the Holy Family surmount the entrance and the modern brick architectural design is highlighted by a large Latin cross and statue of Mary. The lovely modern architecture serves as a tribute to the parishioners who gave so generously to create their historic parish and who have made the parish a viable, thriving entity on Chicago's south side.

Holy Name of Mary, Chicago's first church designed by and for African-Americans, highlights the architecture of Raymond Broady.

The stained glass windows of Holy Name of Mary reflect the black Catholic traditions of the founding members.

The wonderful stone carving of the Holy Family over the entranceway of Holy Name of Mary greets visitors with a comforting presence of the Almighty.

Part V

Historic Immigrant Churches Of Chicago----
An Artist Preserves the Past in Sketches

by

Jack Simmerling

A majestic edifice...attended by
large numbers of faithful.

----*Pope John XXIII*

The Historic Churches of Chicago Collection by Jack Simmerling

1.   St. Ethelreda

2.   Little Flower

3.   St. Cajetan

4.   St. Gabriel

5.   St. Kilian

6.   St. Laurence

7.   St. Margaret of Scotland

8.   Old St. Barnaras

9.   St. Leo

10.   St. Columbanus

11.   St. Philip Neri

12.   St. Sabini

13.   St. Basil

14.   Visitation

15.   Sacred Heart

16.   Holy Family

17.   St. Patrick

18.   Holy Name Cathedral

19.   St. Christina

20.   Christ the King

Saint Ethelreda

Jack Simmerling

Little Flower

Jack Simmerling

Saint Cajetan Church

Jack Simmerling

Saint Gabriel

St. Lawrence

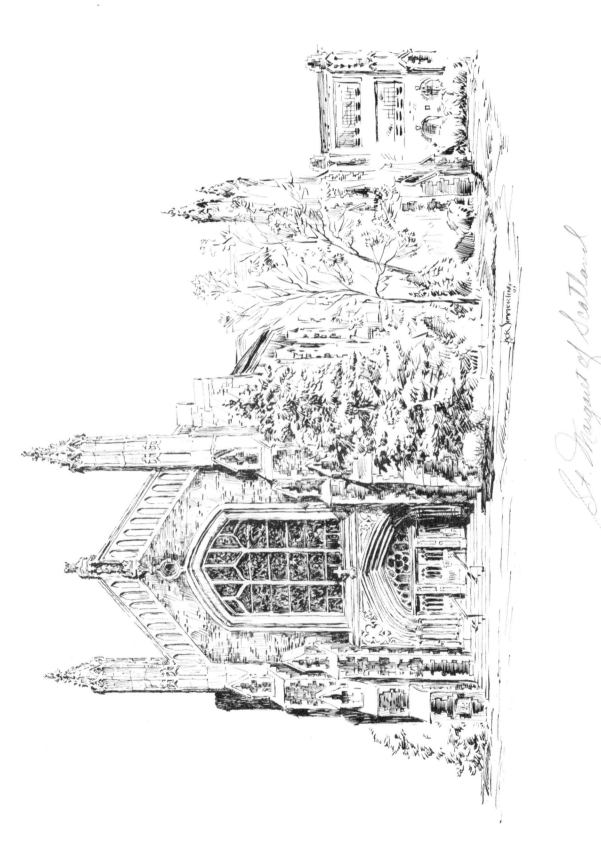

St. Margaret of Scotland

St. Columbanus

ap   Saint Sabina

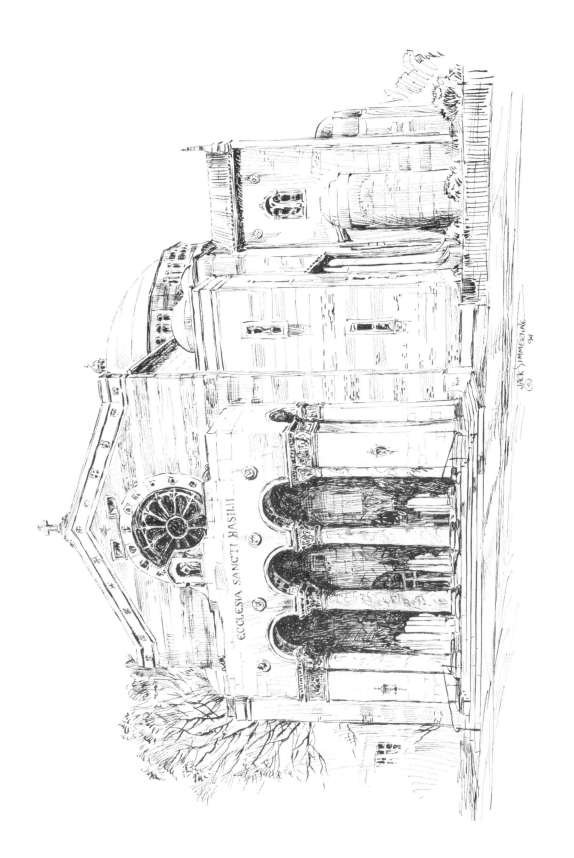

Visitation

Sacred Heart 11657 S. Church

Holy Family Church

213/1000

Jack Simmerling '90

Holy Name

St Christina

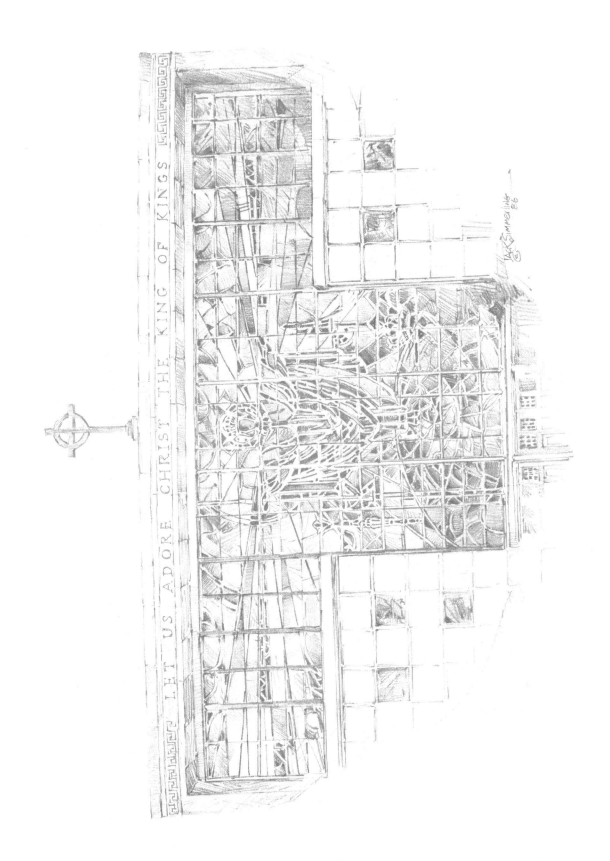